I MADE LEMONADE: A MEMOIR PART ONE

ELA PANDYA

PANDYA PUBLISHING

ALSO BY ELA PANDYA

I Made Lemonade: A Memoir Part One

CONTENTS

To my parents, for without their blessings there would be nothing.

INTRODUCTION
THE BEGINNING

I was born in 1958, a middle sister of two brothers. My parents, Navin and Jashoda, were not well off but worked hard to give us a good education for a better life. My father enjoyed literature and so he gave me a poetic name, Jyotsana, which meant moonlight. But my mother needed a short name for daily use, so I got a second name, Ela. Balancing the cultural expectations, family expectations and their personal ideas of a good future for their family was a constant battle for my parents.

The year and time I was born, Dad acquired a bachelor's in teaching. Mom told me he was ecstatic about both events and repeatedly said I brought him good luck. However, I don't see the logic in that belief. Surely, he did not get his credential instantly, at my birth. I believe he was expressing his joy about having both, his BA and a daughter.

To make our lives better, the struggles and efforts my parents underwent were both heartwarming and heartbreaking. These are the stories of many families in developing nations. But despite the struggles, I truly feel blessed about my father's ability to identify opportunities, and the spirit to take them on, and my mother's ambition, drive and persistence.

My mom and dad helped their respective siblings in their times of need. My maternal grandmother died young, so Grandfather arranged my mother's marriage when she was 17. Oldest of the six children, if married, she would have a home for her younger brothers. Hasmukh, the oldest of them lived with my parents for many years, until Grandfather insisted on arranging his marriage to the sister of the man he wanted to marry my aunt. My aunt was only 13.

My paternal grandparents lived in Isand, a village in Mehsana district of Gujarat. They had a small farm, a few cows and nine children. Grandpa didn't do much due to health problems. His dad, who was a *Mamlatdar* of the *taluka* under British Rule, left behind the resources Grandpa had at his disposal.

A *Mamlatdar* is an executive in charge of a *taluka*, appointed by the British for the sole purpose of revenue management; a *taluka* is similar to a county in the USA.

Grandfather did not have money to pay for his children's education. He paid for the oldest son, Narayan, to go to college. After Uncle Narayan finished college he worked in Baroda.

My dad attended primary school in Isand, after which he attended an Anglo Vernacular school run by the British, for fifth, sixth and seventh grades. For eighth, ninth and tenth grades he needed to attend a school in a neighboring town, Kalol, which was four miles away. Most of Father's friends took the train from Isand to Kalol, but he and his brother walked because they couldn't afford the rail ticket. In monsoons, their friends carried their school bags for them, to keep them from getting wet during their walk to school.

The school in Kalol didn't offer eleventh grade, the

matriculation year, so he went to Baroda, a big city, where his older brother lived and worked. The British established a Bombay University in Baroda, from which father graduated from high school. In 1947, his was the last class to graduate under British rule.

Dad stayed in Baroda, where his younger brother, Ashwin, joined him. When Uncle Narayan had to move to Mehsana due to a job transfer, both brothers found small jobs, like working at a scooter repair shop or giving private tuitions, to pay for rent and college. Sometimes, their uncle, who also lived in Isand, sent them money to make ends meet. Uncle Ashwin wanted to become an engineer while my dad wanted to fulfill his childhood dream of becoming a teacher.

Dad attended two years of college, but it soon became obvious they couldn't afford to pay for the living expenses and tuition for both the brothers. Frustrated, Dad offered to quit college and went back to Isand. He found teaching jobs at various schools in Isand and Kalol and sent money to Uncle Ashwin so he could finish his engineering education. He hoped once Uncle started working at an engineering job he'd get the reciprocal support to finish his education.

While in the engineering college, my uncle received a scholarship to go to Russia for further studies.

During British rule, many wealthy families sent their children to get educated from England. Impressed by the well-fitted shirts and trousers, and conversations in English, it became reputable to have foreign education.

Upon my uncle's return, things didn't go as expected for my father. Uncle enjoyed the attention and respect he got from his status as a foreign-returned engineer. The family, Dad's parents, brothers, and sisters put him in the position of authority in the family. My uncle decided my dad didn't need to study anymore, because he needed to take care of the cows in the village.

The insult and betrayal my dad, married now, felt due to his brother's behavior made a deep impact on him. But, he did not give up his dream. Mom sold her silver jewelry to pay for his tuition, so he accomplished his goal of becoming a teacher.

Along the journey of survival and then progress, Dad became obsessed with the idea that going abroad was the only way to a secure financial future and a higher position in society. His thoughts revolved around finding ways to send us out of India.

This is the story of two ambitious people who dreamt big and had grit to pursue their goals. This is also the story of a father's burning desire to send his children to live a better life in America, and how his impatience and blind love for his grandson affected the journey towards his dream and the outcome for him. It is also a story about the parents' unrealistic expectations from their daughter.

I will try to be as fair and true to the events as my memory permits. Since memories are often based on an individual's perspective at the time of the events, my stories may seem untrue to others. I want to be clear any hurt feelings are not intentional.

CHAPTER ONE

INDIA 1962-63

Ahmedabad

When my mother listened to me repeat the profanities I heard on the streets of the small village, Amreshwar, she immediately started a one-woman protest against living there.

"This small village has one teacher and one doctor. People often pay tuition in the form of vegetables and fruits. My kids are not growing up here. You feel like a king here, but what about their future?"

She won. We moved to Ahmedabad, capital of Gujarat, in 1962, where most of our relatives also lived. We were a family of five. My older brother, Mayank, was born in 1954, when my dad was working in Waghodia. I was born in 1958, in Ahmedabad and my younger brother, Suresh, was born in 1960, in Amreshwar.

Dad found a job in a small school in the area near Mani Nagar.

My parents rented one room in a house nearby. The landlord rented out two rooms, separated by a door, to two different families. Ours was a small, square room, with a water tap and drain in one corner. The toilet was a separate building, behind the house.

Mom had a good sense of making the most of any situation. She was organized and made our room feel like a comfortable home. One corner of the room, by the wall facing the street, became our kitchen with a kerosene stove, a few steel pots and pans, steel dishes and bowls. The windows along that wall provided lighting for cooking, saving on electricity. Along the same wall, by the door, was the water tap and drain, where she hand washed our clothes and dishes.

In the corner adjacent to the kitchen on the other side she stored our bedding, in a neat stack. The mattresses made of cotton fabric covers stuffed with a thin layer of pure cotton, easily foldable, were stacked on a wooden table, along with cotton blankets and pillows. The space below the table offered storage space for storing grains, cooking oil and ghee containers, and even neat stacks of our clothing.

The remaining corner had two folding chairs. If there were more than two visitors, we'd lay out a thick cotton rug on the floor.

Like everyone else, we needed to purchase grains and legumes at the time of harvest. When wheat was available in the market, we'd buy a big sack or two. Until the next season, Mom took out a small bagful of wheat from the big bin and went to the flour mill to have it ground for making *rotis*.

To save money on transporting the big sack in a rickshaw, Mom made arrangements with the grain merchant in the city to allow her to keep the sack in his store. Then, every afternoon she went to the store and filled two small cloth bags with wheat from the sack. She did not want to spend money for the delivery of the big sacks at the time of purchase.

To bring in more money for our family, she attended evening classes to learn sewing. But when my parents realized

Dad would earn more money giving private lessons than what she'd make with sewing jobs, he started tutoring. Mom used her sewing skills to make clothes for us.

Dad was making Rupees (Rs.) 225, of which 75 was spent on rent. Á portion of the rest went to his parents in the village for their sustenance. Tutoring helped a great deal to support our family.

I remember my mother waiting until the last minute to buy things at festival times. At Diwali we watched fireworks from the windows until my parents came home late in the evening with some firecrackers for us.

Despite the shortage of money, Dad enrolled my older brother and me in Nelson English School; a good private school that took pride in training students in conversational English. During recess there were monitors on the campus to enforce the, "Only speak in English" rule. If a student was found speaking in *Gujarati,* our mother tongue, the parent was fined a quarter for every infraction. Mom reminded us, every morning, "Speak in English. I can't afford the fines."

Often Mom needed to leave us home alone while Dad was working or tutoring. She was a dependable and responsible person who was often needed to help with family problems like death, hospital admission, even a disagreement among family members they couldn't resolve on their own. She left my eight-year-old brother to take care of my younger brother and me. Only four years older than me he was a good support for my Mom. We did our homework under his guidance, and played games.

That's when we started calling him, Motabhai, which literally means, older brother. Mom wouldn't allow us to call him by his proper name because it would mean we were disrespecting him.

The school administration where my dad worked kept

changing his shifts, making it difficult for him to continue his private tutoring. When he requested consistency and predictability of schedule, two male teachers who preferred flexibility physically threatened him and ordered him to stop his requests. Dad started looking for another job.

He interviewed for a position at a prestigious school run by Gujarat Law Society. This foundation included many teaching institutions ranging from elementary school to law school. His demonstration lesson so impressed the trustees and the high school administrator he was hired on the spot and began working there in November 1963.

CHAPTER TWO

1963-64

My dad was appointed teacher for the newly started eleventh grade class. He was also assigned to teach English and Geography for the eleventh grade and Social Studies for the fifth and tenth grade classes. In total, he was teaching thirty-five classes.

We still lived in Mani Nagar, seven kilometers from the new job. Dad rode his bicycle to work. Once there, he went up and down the four-story building all day long. The stress of preparing lessons for a wide range of grade levels, the physical strain at school, and biking to work took its toll. He often had an upset stomach and headaches.

In May of 1964, because of Dad's frequent illnesses my parents decided to move to a neighborhood near the new job. The development was called Chandra Colony, a row of houses on two sides of a street, less than a mile long. There were two subdivisions on one side of the Chandra Colony Road. The house we lived in was located in the second one.

My family rented two rooms on the second floor of a two-story house. The landlord used the first floor. They had two boys, one my age and another a year younger. The landlord acquired this house as a dowry when he married our landlady. He did not do much to make a living; he pretended to have a scooter repair service. They were nice people and were excited to have a girl around. I was considered lucky with four brothers to care for me.

The idea of brothers taking care of sisters, because they'd be vulnerable after being sent off to unknown families in marriage, is ingrained in our culture and is reinforced over generations by stories portrayed in Vedic literature and mythologies.

Gujarat Law Society (GLS) Administration and trustees noticed my father's leadership skills and creativity. He was given one of three supervisor positions in addition to his teaching work. In 1966, GLS trustees decided to separate the fifth, sixth and seventh grades. Dad was appointed administrator in charge of the newly formed middle school.

Every promotion meant higher pay, which made my mother happy. She could get wheat delivered to our home.

The school catered to wealthy people and those who appreciated a good education--textile mill owners, judges, corporate leaders, and highly successful business owners. During the yearly high school graduation exams, half of the top-ten highest score achievers were from our school.

Dad was living his dream. He challenged himself and he challenged the students. He focused on academics, but also used his creativity to push the boundaries of what a school could accomplish. He organized annual events unheard of and were never repeated

One year he hosted a *circus*. With the help of physical education (PE) teachers he identified athletic students. Once identified, students trained in various activities like jumping through a ring and gymnastics. The PE teachers gradually grasped his vision, creating excitement in the school.

I walked with him, often very late in the evening, when he'd go to inspect the preparations for the event. Tall canvas tents appeared on the school grounds, under them sat gymnastics equipment. Students practiced their acts. The atmosphere was electric. Dad personally checked the areas for any potential accidents and injuries. The teachers mirrored his emphasis on safety and security asking him jovially to go home and rest. I was proud of my dad.

Other unique events became the talk of the town and made him popular were: a science fair, an Olympic style sports event--complete with someone carrying a torch, parade with flags of various countries, different areas for running, spear and shot-put throwing, the long and short jumps, relay racing and many other competitions.

GLS School was becoming well known and every parent wanted their child to attend. During the hot summer months, Dad and the administration staff worked to screen admission applications, along with potential changes in curriculum with textbooks to match the changes.

There was a steady stream of parents coming to our small home, requesting, and almost begging him, to approve the admission of their children. The administration staff members also showed up to go over and report on the progress of their assignments.

Dad empathized with the desperation of people completely soaked in sweat from the scorching heat outside. He would call to me, "Bring them water, my dear." All day long, it was my job to serve water to every visitor.

Dad loved cold water, but we did not have a refrigerator. In the morning, before the heat took control of the streets, Motabhai or I biked to an ice vendor a mile and a half away, and brought a chunk of ice wrapped in a burlap cloth. Once home, we washed off the sawdust covering the ice, broke it down into small pieces with a big screwdriver and filled up a Styrofoam cooler. When someone came to visit, I'd have to go inside the kitchen, fill up a steel glass with water and add some ice to it. Some days, so many people showed up, my job wore me out.

It was good for Dad, though, he did not like to travel, and this gave him an excuse to not go on a vacation.

Having come up from nothing, Dad believed in equal opportunity for all. Parents with limited income requesting admission of their child showed up, but upon learning about the high tuition, they were disappointed. Dad would look at the transcripts of their child, anyway. If the student's transcripts qualified him or her for admission Dad approved the admission, despite the parent's inability to pay, and then requested the wealthy parents to subsidize the student's tuition.

Dad also loved offering opportunities to the children of extended family, his brothers and sisters, his cousins, even distant relatives. Often we had children of relatives and friends living with us.

From his own experience Dad understood the cycle of poverty too well. Lack of education forces people to work in low paying jobs. This in turn keeps them from affording good education for their children. Many families get caught in this poverty trap, generation after generation. With a strong belief education was a ladder helping one climb out of poverty, he was relentless in finding opportunities for as many young people as possible.

He made me proud. I wanted to do helpful things like him when I grew up.

CHAPTER THREE
1964-70: PART 1

One unexpected benefit of Dad's new job was the children of the employees of the foundation studied in the schools and colleges within its management, at no charge. Dad was earning more salary and there was no tuition expense, so conditions improved drastically for our family.

Motabhai and I started going to school with Dad. It wasn't very far, and the three of us walked to school every day until Dad bought a scooter. Once Motabhai was in high school, he rode his bike to school.

The path we walked from home to get to school led to the back entrance of the compounds. During monsoons, the road was flooded, requiring us to walk in two feet of water. Dad held my hand during those times. There was a covered manhole near the gate to the school from where water was supposed to drain out of the streets. Sometimes, the cover to the two-foot diameter hole was stolen, leaving a huge hole no one could see because of the flooding. Dad made sure students didn't fall into the hole. Either he had a member of the janitorial staff stand by it or he stood by it. He made sure every child left safely for their home after school before we left.

Motabhai thrived at the new school. Hardworking and sincere, he scored well in all his classes and became a favorite of the teachers. I often heard them telling my dad how great his son did in their class.

Once, as I sat outside Dad's office waiting to walk home with him, I heard my dad and one of the teachers talk.

"Pandit Sir, Mayank is a good student. He has the potential to rank first in the State Board exams. He will get into medical school, no doubt."

I didn't hear Dad speak. He was a man of few words. Then I heard the teacher continue, "What do you think about Ela? You think she'll ever do as well as her brother?"

Again, Dad gave no response.

It didn't bother me everyone thought Motabhai was the best, because he was. Even after Mom made him supervise us doing math problems during summer vacation, I couldn't become as proficient in math as he was.

Dad wanted Motabhai to go to medical school and then go to America for the rest of his life. Without any sibling or parent in America to sponsor us, this was the only way to accomplish his goal. America was offering entry permits and visas to medical professionals. His expectations of Motabhai were not a secret. Both Mom and Dad thought once he went to America, we'd follow.

My grandparents--Dada and Dadi, were getting old and it became clear to the family they couldn't be left alone in the village. Since the time when my uncle refused to help my dad finish his education, the two brothers did not speak, so it was informally decided the grandparents would live with each of the three brothers for four months at a time. When they stayed with Uncle Ashwin, if either one of them got sick, he put them in a rickshaw to our house.

Dad's older brother's wife had a combative nature and

yelled at his sisters when they visited their parents. So, my grandparents didn't like to stay with them.

My parents ended up carrying the majority of the responsibility for my paternal grandparents until it came to a point they stayed with us permanently. Though angry at the unfairness of the situation, my Mom had a kind heart and could not see them suffer.

The situation used to put a strain on our financial and emotional resources. Mom and Dad argued often because Mom wanted Dad's siblings to appreciate and respect her and Dad, for the sacrifices they made as a family. But to Dad's family, Uncle Ashwin, was still the most important person; after all, he received education from abroad. His sisters and brothers refused to take sides or talk to my uncle to help share responsibilities.

Once members of Dad's family gathered to talk things out. But, because the two brothers harbored much anger it was impossible for them to have a normal conversation.

I know my mother was angry with Uncle Ashwin because he tore up the pictures from Motabhai's *Janoi,* instead of handing them over to my parents.

Janoi is a symbolic ceremony signifying the initiation of a young boy into the educational phase of his life. In ancient times, when the sons became old enough to go to school, they were sent to the forest to live at the guru's ashram and learn from him the wisdom and knowledge that had been passed on since Vedic times. Over the generations, it became a ritual celebrating the age when a boy became old enough to go to school.

My father loved taking family pictures. He did not mind spending on pictures of my brother's *Janoi* ceremony. When my parents asked my uncle to give them the pictures, he responded, "Who are you going to show them to, the cows?" When Mom insisted she get the pictures, he tore them up.

Motabhai appeared for his Secondary School Certification exam held by Gujarat Education Board. He'd finish high school and start college. Mom and Dad were certain he'd make the list of top ten scores in the state. On the day results were announced, we couldn't wait to see his name in the newspaper.

The newspaper arrived. The first name on the list wasn't his. His name didn't show up on the list at all. It was a devastating blow to him and Dad. Mom cried. Motabhai cried. Father was stone cold and quiet. If he had tears in his eyes, we couldn't see them.

When we saw his score sheet, it showed he was in the 74th percentile. To get admission in medical school he needed to be in the 98th percentile and to be in engineering school he needed to be between 80th and 90th percentile. His scores were shockingly low and incomprehensible. How could that be?

The answers were evaluated by teachers who offered to do extra work during the summer. It was not possible to find out who evaluated my brother's answers in every subject.. Some rich parents bribed the administration staff at schools to find out who got the bundle of tests, which included their children's responses. Then they'd find the teacher and visit them to offer a bribe for giving higher scores to their children. Dad's principles of honesty and integrity wouldn't allow him to do the same. Even if he was desperate enough to want to do so, we didn't have enough money. It was a sad moment for our family.

CHAPTER FOUR

1964-70: PART 2

During hot summers when Dad was not receiving parents wanting admissions and school staff wanting signatures on orders for school books and such, we'd go to the movies. The theaters were air-conditioned. Watching a movie gave us three hours of respite from the hot, humid summers. Sometimes, Dad would make us watch two movies, back to back. By the time we left the theater it would be past sundown. Returning home in the rickshaw would be tolerable.

It wasn't just he wanted to stay out of the heat. He loved movies. He took the three of us, my brothers and me, to watch foreign films, like *Dr. Zhivago, The Eagle has Landed, Where Eagles Dare, Hatari,* and *The Dirty Dozen,* to name a few. We did not understand the dialogues but we liked them because they were different from the Indian films.

"In the future everyone will need to know how to speak in English. Pay attention, watch and learn." He instructed us many times.

Every summer cousins from the maternal side or paternal side came to live with us. Or, we went to spend the summer at an aunt's or an uncle's home, from either side of the family.

My youngest maternal aunt, Nirumasi's daughter, Gita, was born two days before me. Nirumasi's family lived in the village of Dhamasana. Her husband, Shantilal Masa, had a farm and four buffaloes. The buffaloes were given names, and we'd try talking with them.

Life with them was very different from life in Ahmedabad. We'd go to the farm with Shantilal Masa, on his bullock cart. Sometimes when the pump was on, he let us play in the water coming out of the ground in big water lines. We'd jump into the concrete collection tank and watch water flow into the farms. One time, we saw large stacks of hay on the farm. They looked shiny and soft from a distance. Suresh, my younger brother, and I didn't know what they were. And without asking, Suresh jumped into the stack. Later he was very itchy, but the locals had a good laugh.

What I loved most about going to Nirumasi's house was the morning breakfast. She made thick flat bread, *bhakhri*, from red wheat flour. Her husband, and his brothers, and the farmers, ate those before going to the farm. After they left, we'd get to eat *bhakhri* and tea. The whole-wheat flour from red wheat had a sweetness to it. I didn't taste in the wheat flour in the city. I loved *bhakhris* made from it. Masi was amused.

Shantilal Masa was a professional cook. He and his brother prepared many meals for the lunches and dinners at the family weddings, or religious ceremonies, like *janoi*. His *daal, made* from dried split pigeon peas, was famous. No one could duplicate the taste. He also made really tasty *fulwadi*, a deep-fried snack made with chick-pea flour and a special blend of spices. A Gujarati meal was never complete without it.

Nirumasi's neighbors were curious about the kids from the city. They would laugh at us for not knowing normal things about village life, but were fascinated with our speech and mannerisms. They were especially intrigued by the fact we knew the English language. They'd make me stand on a wooden bench to sing a song or speak something in English. When I sang *Twinkle Twinkle Little Stars* and *Baa Baa Black sheep,* they clapped, in awe.

Some summers I'd stay with my paternal aunt, Shobha Foi. Her daughter Hema was two years younger than me, and her son Jayesh was two years younger than Motabhai. The four of us were good friends.

Hema was very creative, artistic and talented, which I was not. Mother would tell Hema to make me do art projects with her, when I went to stay with them. I did not have patience for meticulously sticking beads or sequins on the outlined image of God or Goddess, or sitting in one place making cross stitches on a tablecloth.

Shobha Foi and her husband were conservative and old-fashioned, so as a girl Hema was trained in doing all the housework from a young age. Hema thought I was cool, because I could speak in English and was outgoing, not bashful like her. We adored each other. I also adored her brother, Jayeshbhai. He went to school for diploma engineering courses at a school near our house. They lived in Mani Nagar, seven kilometers from us. So, he often stayed with us in Chandra Colony. He'd help me with homework, and during the college and MBA years he'd help me with projects and presentations.

Some summers, my Mom would invite Gita and Hema to stay with us. That made it even more fun. The three of us would go to the movies, go to Law Garden for ice cream, and play cards.

Then, there were summers when all the children on the

maternal side went to stay with Hasmukh Mama (a generic term for Mom's brother) in his one room rental. He was not well off financially, but he was rich at heart. Savita Mami (a generic term used to imply Mom's brother's wife) never complained about having to spend their meager resources on feeding all of us.

CHAPTER FIVE
1964-70: PART 3

The Hindi movies had four or five songs. Most of the songs were duets, sung by the lead male and female characters, expressing their undying love for each other. Sometimes, it was just one of them singing of the other's betrayal, or lamenting about separation from the other due to societal norms. When they sang happy songs they danced to its beat. Sometimes, there were devotional songs and the female lead character performed a classical dance.

When we got home from the movies, I danced the way the heroine in the movie did. I remembered the steps to the dance, which impressed my parents. In 1968, they made me happy when they enrolled me in classical Indian dancing classes run by Ilaben Thaker.

The dance studio was four miles from our home. Initially, I took a bus to the classes. But, as I grew older I was allowed to bike there. Three times a week, my class was at seven p.m. and lasted forty-five minutes. This meant I had to leave home a little before six-thirty and be back by a little after eight-thirty. It was perfect. I had time to finish homework before leaving for the dance class.

In my class, I met a girl named Jigisha, who lived near me. Our parents were happy, we could watch out for each other on the bike rides to and from the class. We talked a lot during those rides, making it seem much shorter.

It was inevitable, once in a while one of us missed the class and the other would have to go alone. Those rides were very boring. The lonely ride back became even a bigger problem during the dark winter evenings.

There was a patch about a mile long, on our route that was scary and sparse. It was along the college grounds. Hence, there were no people, lights, homes or other signs of life. There were not many vehicles on that road, either. We would try to ride quickly to get out of the area.

On one such cold, winter evening, Jigisha was not able to come to the class. I was riding back from class. I was scared but I never did like to admit it. My parents did not know my friend was not with me. I was biking as fast as I possibly could.

A man about thirty years old passed by on his two-wheel Vespa. He glanced at me and kept going. I didn't think much of it. In a few minutes, another man drove by on his Vespa. Again, I didn't think much of it. In a few minutes yet another man drove by.

I always paid attention to the road and people around me, especially on that road.

When I noticed it was the same man who passed by, I concluded I might be in trouble.

When he realized I had noticed what he was doing, he came back one more time, slowed next to my bike and started chatting with me. To a stranger, it would seem like a couple of friends going together, enjoying each other's company.

Pretending to be friendly, I tried not to let him know I was terrified. I was also thinking. I needed to lose him before he did something bad to me. Many other thoughts came to me.

"What if I started shouting and waving at someone driving by?" I wondered. I rejected the idea thinking to myself, "Nah, no one would listen and stop. On a cold, dark evening, people want to get home as fast as possible. I might just make this man think I understood what he was doing and make him behave more aggressively." I went on analyzing some more. "What if he was just being nice and riding with me to protect me?"

As I brainstormed through the ideas, we moved forward in the direction of my home. I hoped at some point, his path would be different than mine and he would drive away.

He did not.

Finally, we reached the turn entering my Chandra Colony neighborhood. Unfortunately, my home was at the far end. As I turned onto the road, he brought his scooter in front of me and stopped.

He commanded, "Let's go. You can go with me on my scooter. Leave the bike here." He guessed I had come close to my home and knew he had to make his move.

No one I knew from the neighborhood was entering the area and passing by me. There was no one around. I was going to have to go with him. If I refused, he would grab me and leave. My parents would never know what happened to me. I could barely breathe. I felt as if my life was going to end.

Then, my instinct kicked in. "My parents don't care what I do, as long as they know what I am doing," I told him, hoping he believed me. "I don't mind going with you, let me go inform my parents."

Although I tried this idea, I feared he was not going to believe me. If he touched me, he would know I was shaking with fear.

"Ok, I will wait. Come back quickly." He replied.

At first, I didn't believe he trusted what I said. As I recovered from the shock of hope I said, "I will be right back."

I didn't want to make him suspicious, so I walked calmly as he watched me. The first house I came to, I opened the gate, went to the front door and knocked hard, figuring the bad man did not know it wasn't my house. If I walked all the way to my house, he might get impatient and come after me.

"Who is it?" Uncle Ranjit yelled out.

"It's me, Ela," I answered, "Please hurry."

He sensed the panic in my voice and opened the door.

I told him the story as fast as I could.

"Where is this guy? Where is your bike? How dare your parents let you go by yourself like this? I am going to have a word with them." He was angry and worried.

"He is waiting for me. If I take too long, he will come for me." I reminded him of the urgency of the situation.

Uncle calmed down and grabbed my arm, "Let's go. Take me to him."

We walked to the spot where this stranger was waiting for me. Uncle gestured as if he was about to beat this man up and started talking to him, angrily, "How dare you harass young girls like this? Wait, let me have your name so I can report you to the police or better yet, I will have my sons beat you up."

The stranger got on his scooter and drove away in a hurry, without looking back.

"He's gone. Come on, let's go. Get your bike. I want to go with you to your home." He commanded. The whole time we walked together, he kept muttering angry words about my parents and the stranger.

When we reached my home, my parents let me in as usual. Then they saw Uncle Ranjit behind me and welcomed him with a surprised look. Before they could ask the purpose of his visit he started talking.

"How dare you let a young girl go all by herself?" He questioned my parents.

My parents tried to explain they didn't know.

We were all in trouble now. Uncle was upset with my parents and me. My parents were upset with me.

The discussion about the gravity of the situation went on for a while. When all the grownups were satisfied with the discussion, they turned to me. I didn't think there was much more left to discuss. It was more like they needed to recover from the "what ifs" of the situation.

"Oh no, now what did I do?" I wondered.

"You are a very smart and brave girl," they said to me.

I was sure I was going to be informed about the punishment for not telling my parents, so I was surprised at what they said, instead. They told me how they were proud of how I had protected myself. The night ended with a lot of advice for the future.

"From now on, neither one of you goes alone to the class." Dad said. "I will also speak with Jigisha's parents regarding this."

I understood.

CHAPTER SIX

1970-74: PART 1

Suresh, my younger brother, was a handful. He was mischievous, clever and hard to control. Mom and Dad were at their wits end, trying to figure out how to make him care for schoolwork.

If he found himself in trouble, he dashed out of the house and down the steep, slippery concrete stairs, so fast no one was able to catch him.

At school, teachers complained about him. Dad gave them permission to treat him like any other student and not to be partial towards him just because he was the principal's son. He'd even suggest they make him clean bathrooms or sweep floors.

Neighborhood mothers frequently came to our home to complain about something he did while playing with their children. Once, at the instigation of his friends, he threw a handful of dirt on a scooter driver. The poor driver couldn't see and had to stop on the side to clean his eyes. He was angry and ran after Suresh. Suresh ran into a neighbor's house and went out the back door. The homeowners never saw him come and go, but the scooter-driver reprimanded them for raising an unruly child. The perplexed homeowners did not say much. The scooter-driver left in a huff.

Mom was very strict, always trying to teach us discipline. She recruited my older brother, Mayank, as her enforcer. My younger brother, Suresh and I were not happy about it.

On a particularly wet monsoon day, Mom and Dad had to run errands so they were gone on Dad's scooter. I think, deep down, they enjoyed going out in the rain. After three months of sweltering and moist heat of triple-digit temperatures, it was fun to go out and get wet in the rain. If I had been an adult and hadn't needed to ask anyone's permission, I would have been out and about in the rain, as well.

But we were kids. Mayank was about fifteen, Suresh nine and a half and I was about eleven years old. We were stuck at home.

"Make sure they eat only four *puris*," Mom instructed our brother, who we were supposed to address as Motabhai. "One must have discipline in everything. Sleepiness and hunger grow as much as you allow them to grow." I heard her say it many times.

Puris are a smaller version of the flat bread in India. Unlike the bigger version, *Puris* are always deep fried in peanut oil. They can be plain, with only salt added to it, or they can be spicy with turmeric, salt, and red crushed pepper. *Puris* can be soft, made to mold around a spoonful of cooked vegetables. Or made crispy, which made for a great after-school snack with yogurt or just by themselves.

"Who does he think he is?" Suresh muttered under his breath, "I can eat as much as I want."

I didn't want to eat more, but I did agree with him.

He asked for more *puris*. It was more of an order than a request.

"Mom said four, so I cannot give you more. She said she

will be home soon so she doesn't want you to ruin your dinner," he said loyally.

Suresh stopped fidgeting and walked into the kitchen. Motabhai and I couldn't see what he was doing because there was a heavy orange and white striped fabric curtain between the two rooms. Mom had made the curtain on her rickety sewing machine. Suresh was there long enough to make *Motabhai* suspicious of him.

"Suresh, how long does it take to have a drink of water?"

"Almost done. I'll be right there. I was very thirsty." Suresh fibbed.

He didn't come out soon. The enforcer was getting suspicious, "I know what you are doing. You are eating more *puris.*" He was walking towards the kitchen as he spoke.

He found Suresh drinking water. They both walked out of the kitchen together as Motabhai was saying, "It does not take this long to drink water, I know you were eating *puris.*"

They both settled down in their spots. Motabhai was the only one with a desk in one corner of the room. Being the oldest and a very good student, he deserved a desk. Suresh and I used a study desk with short legs and a slanted top, similar to what Gandhi used. The table slid over our stretched out legs, reaching the stomach, making it comfortable to have a book on it. Suresh conveniently settled with his desk, on the wall by the door to the kitchen.

I noticed Motabhai eyeing Suresh every few minutes to see if he was chewing on something.

Suresh was indeed squirming and acting as if he had broken some rule. He looked like he was trying to break a piece of *puri* from his pocket.

"I knew it. I knew it," Motabhai exclaimed as he sprinted towards Suresh.

Before he could reach, Suresh shot towards the entrance

door and ran, more like hopped down the wet, concrete staircase, Motabhai at his heels.

The staircase was steep and narrow. Only one person could go down at a time. I watched them and screamed, "Stop it, stop it, you two. Mom will be angry if she finds out you were fighting."

By the time Suresh reached the bottom of the staircase, Motabhai had caught up with him. He grabbed Suresh by the arm and tried to check his pockets.

"I know you have *puris* in your pocket. Let me check."

The heavy rain was sheeting down, making everything slippery and unsafe. The repeat use of stairs for many years had smoothed out the concrete steps, making them dangerous in the rain. The landing was not very large, beyond was just ground which had turned into a muddy goop.

Both of them were drenched with rain. Motabhai's eyeglasses were so covered with water, I wondered if he could see anything. There was not a soul in sight, on either side of the house.

"I didn't take any *puris*," Suresh repeated. He squirmed so much it was impossible for Motabhai to get his hand in his pockets.

I stood there watching both of them, crying. I always cried when my brothers fought. I knew both of them very well. I knew Suresh was capable of doing what *Motabhai* was accusing him of. My little brother was very smart and naughty, always pushing the limits, testing everyone in authority. I also knew, *Motabhai*, being the oldest and trusted by mother, wouldn't let Suresh get away with whatever he thought Suresh had done.

Suddenly, something totally unexpected happened, something none of us imagined.

A few *puris* fell on the ground. It looked like they came out from the bottom of Suresh's pocket. If music were playing at the time, it would have stopped.

Without flinching a bit, Suresh spoke, "The crow dropped them."

Motabhai was furious. He dragged Suresh up the stairs. The minute they got into the house, they engaged into a fistfight, while I sat in the corner crying.

"Mom and Dad have so many problems already. Why do you have to add to their problems? Stop fighting."

I loved both of them deeply and couldn't see them hurting each other.

Being his older sister, I protected Suresh fiercely when he got in trouble, but it wasn't just him I was protecting. My parents didn't need more stress in their lives.

On Sundays, *Motabhai* and his friends played cricket in the streets. I wanted to play, but the boys refused to allow girls to play. I knew *Motabhai* didn't mind, but he wasn't able to make his friends change the rules.

My mother, a strong believer in equality, showed up one Sunday and insisted they allow me to play with them. They couldn't argue with an adult. After that, I started playing cricket.

CHAPTER SEVEN
1970-74: PART 2

It was my first year of high school. Motabhai was studying science courses at St. Xavier's College. I was a curious kid and asked him many questions and he had an answer for every one of my questions.

In our two-room home, Motabhai and I slept in the family room. The room had two twin-size wooden beds, which served as a sofa during the day, and beds for my brother and me at night. It was a ritual, changing sheets every morning and night.

"Say *Aum Namah Shivay, Aum Namah Shivay* and go to sleep," were Mom's standard instructions at the end of the day.

Lord Shiva, the Hindu God manifests himself in a human form, as well as a *linga*, a black rock post with a rounded top. He is considered to be the destroyer of ignorance and the symbol of "what is possible, the potential." He was our family deity of choice. Mom advised we chant his name and slide into fearless and peaceful slumber.

The living room windows opened into the narrow landing,

and had a clear view of the sky. Although the window was made of iron bars in a wooden frame, I was afraid to sleep by the window. Motabhai slept in the bed and I on the bed on the opposite wall. Some days, he would look at the sky and talk about the stars and the moon. I loved listening to everything he said.

One such starry night, the moon was full. Mom had just left us with her standard instructions. He uttered, "The moon looks beautiful tonight."

Mom's words about praying to God and brother's words about the sky triggered a curiosity in me. I asked, "So, Motabhai, did God make the moon?"

"I don't know, maybe."

"But you are studying science, you know there is no such thing as God."

"Well, no one has seen God but it didn't mean he doesn't exist."

"Tell me, if God made the universe, where did he stand to make it? I mean, wouldn't he need a platform or a desk or something?"

"Hinduism says, when Brahma opens his eyes everything exists, and when he closes his eyes, it goes away."

"Really? You believe that? I am so confused. I think scientists know how the universe began. They can explain to us there is no such thing as God, a person, who stood in nothing and made everything."

Amused, Motabhai said something that, perhaps he didn't know, would impact me as much as it did. "Scientists are trying to figure it out, but they don't know yet."

My heart sank. I couldn't comprehend the idea that scientists and my Motabhai didn't know how the world began. My mind raced a mile a minute. My stomach felt queasy, I was in total shock. All my hopes were shattered. I wanted to believe as I got older, I'd learn how it all began, things that have been sorted out and discovered already. The prospect of not ever getting to know was not something I could grapple with. No one had seen God, and scientists didn't know anything. I was afraid I'd never find out.

CHAPTER EIGHT

1970-74: PART 3

Because of the reputation of GLS as a successful and coveted Institution, a team of educators from Pestalozzi Children's Village in England visited our school. A charitable institution established to provide education and a better future to the children who suffered due to World War II, Pestalozzi Children's Village later expanded to include children from developing countries.

They intended to administer a test to the students of fifth and sixth grades. They'd offer to take three or four students, who scored well on the test, to England for further education at Pestalozzi Children's Village.

Dad welcomed them with great enthusiasm. He wanted to host a test at our school, but none of the parents allowed their children to take the test. "We can afford to send our children abroad when they are older. Eleven is too young to send them away."

Dad's pride was injured. His school was not the one sending students for free education abroad. Dad and the administrator of GLS High School, Amin Sir, talked about it and thought of sending their sons for the test. Since they couldn't host it, they had the head of the custodian staff of our school, Babar, take Suresh and Rohit, Amin Sir's son, to Baroda, the next big city in Gujarat.

Suresh and Rohit, both eleven years old, performed extremely well. Both dads decided to send their sons to England.

Mom did not like the idea. Just like other parents of our school, she believed it was too tender an age to send a child away. She tried to reason with Dad. "What if he gets sick?"

She cried and argued until she no longer could.

Dad explained, "He wants to go. Why are you getting in the way of his bright future? When he blames you you'll regret not allowing him to go."

"He is too young to know what's good for him." Mom pleaded, but it didn't matter.

Suresh and Rohit left for England in 1972.

Mom went into deep depression. I often saw her wiping her tears while doing her chores. She was angry with Dad and barely spoke with him. She did not want to make anything Suresh liked to eat. She was in a state of panic and wasn't able to sleep. Our family doctor had to prescribe Valium so her brain could rest at night.

I was also sad. I missed him. We were the silly brother-sister pair who loved laughing. Often, when someone was visiting, he'd make faces and imitate their mannerisms. Even if I tried to look away, I couldn't stop laughing. I'd run to the kitchen to avoid disrespecting the guest. He followed me to the kitchen. Mom got annoyed at us every time.

Motabhai, my older brother, was the serious type and the enforcer of Mom's rules, when she wasn't home. It was a different type of relationship. He was an authority figure. He made us do homework and extra work. He stopped us from eating more snacks than what Mom had rationed. Upset with him, Suresh and

I would protest by telling him, "We are not going to call you Motabhai." We repeated his first name again and again, instead of calling him Motabhai, to show him disrespect.

The event of two eleven-year-old boys going away from home was big news. Various organizations held programs to honor them. Two little boys in suits sitting on a dais, whispering, and laughing, when the adults kept talking about them, was a strange sight. They even met a famous female actor, Nargis Dutt!

While Dad was hopeful Motabhai would become a doctor and go to America, he was delighted through Suresh he had found another door out of India. He hosted a reception, an ice-cream party, on our street. He invited every person he knew—relatives, friends, colleagues, and school staff. Suresh and Rohit wore suits and sat on a sofa, while guests walked up to them and blessed them. Dad stood next to the sofa and requested the guests not leave without having ice cream. His face beamed with pride and joy.

Though we missed Suresh, our lives in India had to go on. Motabhai went to college to major in Zoology because it was a back door entrance to medical college.

Because of Motabhai's college tuition and my grandparents' healthcare, I saw my parents struggling to make ends meet. Often there were arguments about having to spend money on the social obligations at the ceremonies of his sisters. "Your sisters love Ashwin. Why can't he pay for the saree at your sister's baby shower?"

Every time, Mom would first refuse to pay for whatever it was. She'd tell my dad to ask other brothers to contribute. They'd refuse and in the end to fulfill their obligations, mother would pawn her jewelry for cash or Dad would take a loan from GLS Foundation. They became good at juggling loans from the bank or from the wealthy friends Dad made because of his job.

In the newspapers I read articles about a lady named Ela Bhatt. She was an attorney advocating for enacting protective laws for self-employed women. While helping the unions of women textile mill workers she learned the women did not make enough money for their livelihood, which required them to undertake side businesses for additional income. They sold vegetables at street corners, fresh flowers outside the temples, or even went door-to-door on Sundays, collecting old newspapers they could sell for recycling. Ela Bhatt noticed while the women were protected under the labor laws, for their regular jobs, there were no legal protections and support for the unregistered side jobs. Hence women faced exploitation and harassment from various government agencies. She started a trade union of these women, the Self Employed Women's Association, SEWA. Ela Bhatt impressed me so much, I read everything published about her in the newspapers.

I was in tenth grade in 1973, ready to graduate from high school, in April of 1974. Wanting to be like Motabhai, I opted for difficult electives like physics and chemistry.

In December of 1973, students all over Gujarat united to protest against the corrupt state government. Schools and colleges shut down. Big masses of students marched daily to the governor's office.

I joined the protests. I had to be a part of something big.

Dad believed as retaliation to the protests, the State Education Minister would announce the dates for the School Board Exams without prior notice.

Dad tried to warn me. "Eli, keep studying or you'll not pass high school. We can't trust politicians."

Dad was right. The government announced the dates for Board Exams.

I wasn't ready.

It was impossible to prepare for physics and chemistry exams in a short time. In the application form for the exams, I dropped both and opted to appear for social studies.

"I warned you. I'm not going to guide you." Dad said with a straight face.

I begged, "But this is your subject. Please, Dad."

He replied, "No." He pretended to be upset, but a slight smile, like of the Mona Lisa, gave him away. Still, he did not tutor me.

I studied hard and for long hours. The long Indian history starting from 3300 BCE made it difficult to remember the dates of the historical events. From the start of Mauryan empire, to when East India Company arrived in India, to the first university established and who started it, including dates and causes of the Jallianwala Bagh massacre, and so on. But, I persisted.

I passed my High School Boards with a 73% score and had the second highest score in social studies at our school.

I teased Dad. "What do you teach your students? Look, I scored more than all of them, except one."

He gave me his Mona Lisa smile.

CHAPTER NINE

1974-78

Since I opted out of science courses, I couldn't go to a science college. Dad suggested I study for a BA in English. "There's going to be a great need for teachers of English. You'll do well."

I didn't want to be a teacher and live a life of meager resources. I decided to go for business and commerce courses.

Dad and I went together to apply for admission at H.A. College of Commerce (HA). The clerk at the admissions window took one look at my mark sheet, looked up and told my Dad, "Saheb, she will easily get into H.L College of Commerce (HL), the top college."

"Yes, I know, but she insists on coming here."

HL ranked number one among the commerce colleges within Gujarat. HA was the second best. I chose HA because it belonged in the GLS group of institutions; Dad wouldn't have to pay tuition.

I didn't share my motivation to go for the second best college with my Dad. I was trying to help my parents where they hurt the most, financially.

This wasn't the first time I made a choice based on what

was best for our family's finances. When I finished seven years of my Bharat Natyam training, in 1976, I didn't participate in the Arangetram, a program parents host as a formal graduation ritual.

Arangetram involves giving gifts of silk sarees to the female members and scarves to the male members of the team of singers and musicians. They would accompany me on the stage while I performed dances all evening long. Renting the auditorium, formally inviting family and friends and serving refreshments was also a part of the parents' responsibility. I refused to do my *Arangetram*. "It's not like I need the certificate for my career," I argued.

During the four years when Motabhai was studying Zoology at St. Xavier's Science College, Gujarat State Education Board decided to discontinue the policy of allowing Zoology graduates to enter medical school.

It was another devastating blow to my father's dream. Although Motabhai graduated with good scores, it felt like a failure. Motabhai never wanted a career in Zoology, he chose to study it only because it would've helped him to get into a medical school. Now that door was closed and his feelings of loss of four years of his life were palpable. My parents blamed his bad luck for the way he faced one disappointment after another. They often uttered, "Poor child, he has very bad stars."

I felt sad for Motabhai.

While at college, he fell in love with a Christian girl. They first came to know each other, as chemistry lab partners. They found support in their mutual dreams of becoming doctors.

When Mom found out, she ordered him to stop talking to the girl.

My parents worked hard to gain respect and social status in the family and in the Brahmin community. Their son marrying a Christian girl would shatter their image. They were not about to let that happen.

Dad frantically looked for a Brahmin girl and, against Mom's protests, arranged my brother's engagement with Disha, a girl from a Brahmin family.

Mom thought Motabhai deserved better. In her judgment, this girl did not match our family's culture and ideology. What was worse was she was a first cousin of Uncle Ashwin's wife. Mom worried Disha would tear our family apart, similar to what her cousin did with my Dad's family. The two brothers, who were also best friends, lost their closeness after my uncle's marriage.

In a short time, Motabhai endured two setbacks. He became even more withdrawn. He couldn't relate to Disha. After the formal engagement, he didn't want to go out with her. Disha and my parents pushed me to join them for a movie or a dinner, to help break the ice. Gradually, his demeanor softened, but there was always a sense of sadness about him.

Not knowing what direction to take for his career, he took a job as a Pharmaceutical Representative. The job involved a lot of traveling, giving him time to be by himself, which suited him. His work ethic and sincerity helped him do well. Within a short time, he was transferred to the Valsad-Navsari area of South Gujarat, close to Bombay. He was in a higher position and in charge of a larger territory.

I sensed the conflict both my parents felt between the happiness of their son and the honor they craved among their peers. Mom missed him after he left for Navsari and somehow his absence made the sense of guilt stronger.

In 1976, my younger brother Suresh visited from England, after four years. The excitement was beyond measure. My mother couldn't contain her joy. I brought out my container full of candy I'd saved for the last four years, and shared it with him.

Suresh had changed completely. He grew tall and skinny. His hair was long, reaching down to his shoulders. He didn't speak Gujarati and felt awkward with us, as if we were strangers.

At Pestalozzi, Suresh lived with other boys and a housefather, in the India House for Boys. There was also an India house and a housemother for the girls. Once the students left their home country, they weren't allowed to call home. They attended local schools and participated in festivals and programs hosted by their House.

In a few days, he went back to finish high school. Once again, we had to live through the loss of a son and a brother.

The program required after high school, they went back to their home country or, if they wanted to stay in England, they went to college at their own expense. Watching him during his visit, I wondered if he'd like to come back to India. He seemed out of place.

His visit was during the rainy season. Valsad, where Motabhai worked, was flooded. Suresh and I took a train to Valsad to help him evacuate and brought him home. We laughed a lot during those three days. It felt like the old days. Suresh felt more comfortable with us, which made the three days we shared memorable.

Soon after he returned to England, the Pestalozzi Program dismissed him. The explanation for his removal from the program was not clear. My Dad was told he broke house rules despite multiple warnings and lost his privilege to continue to be there. He left England and came back to us.

He didn't like to be in India. He couldn't relate to anyone, couldn't talk to anyone. Feeling lost, he cried often. Father took him around to visit the best colleges and schools. They failed to impress him.

Dad's sister, Manufoi, lived in England. Her husband offered to take Suresh in, with an understanding Dad would repay him for the expenses they'd incur for keeping him. Financially, it was beyond my father's ability to afford his son's education abroad. But, Suresh's future mattered more. My parents put on a brave face and sent him to England, one more time.

Tired of traveling, Motabhai quit his job. He appeared for the test held by a national bank for an entry-level position. There was no doubt he'd do well. He started working at a bank in Ahmedabad.

Since the engagement, Disha's family brought up the wedding a few times. They were afraid if Motabhai rejected their daughter, after a long engagement, it would cast doubts about their daughter's personality and character and hurt her chances of ever getting married. But my Mom believed a man shouldn't be married until he was able to support his wife and family. She stood her ground.

Now that Motabhai was back with us and had a stable job, Disha's dad brought up Motabhai and Disha's marriage. The wedding took place in May of 1978.

Even after renting one more room on the same floor, our home seemed inadequate for the newlyweds. Dad's friend, who was a senior officer in Gujarat government, was allotted a flat in the government-housing program for state employees. Since he already lived in his own house he didn't need the flat, so he suggested Motabhai and Bhabhi (generic term for brother's wife) move to the flat.

To keep the expenses down, my parents decided we maintain only one kitchen. Both of them came every morning to our home for lunch, before going to work.

CHAPTER TEN
1978-80

I graduated from college with a Bachelor's in Commerce. I scored the highest in the University (which included many commerce colleges) in the subject of business management. A professor of business administration at HL College of Commerce who was also a humor columnist, Bakul Tripathi, evaluated my answers. He kept my answer sheets to share them with his future students. After many years of HL ranking first at the university, HA Commerce College took that spot. The GLS Board of Trustees put my name on the honor list on a wall in HA College.

"What's next?" Dad asked while patting me on my back. Whenever he was proud and happy with someone, he'd pat on the back and with a loud, encouraging voice ask questions or congratulate them, his mouth wide open with a grin. His pride was visible.

Well known and well liked in the city and among the GLS community, he received comments and compliments about my results, which he enjoyed thoroughly.

"Like Motabhai, I'll try for a bank job," I told him.

"You did well in the business management course. I've

heard Gujarat University has recently started a master's program in business management."

Traditionally, businesses and factories were family owned, passed down through the generations. The concept of an actual team of management with formal education in business, accounting, marketing, human resources, purchasing, inventory management, and taxation, did not exist.

Inspired by the Indian Institute of Management, a world-renowned school of management, where students and instructors came from all over the world, Gujarat University started the B.K. School of Management.

"You should go for an MBA," he suggested.

Expecting him to arrange my marriage soon, I was surprised.

"Your professors at HA suggested it."

"Are you sure?" I was in disbelief. "You are not going to arrange my marriage?"

"I will not talk about your marriage until you say so," he assured me.

I biked to the school to pick up an application form and realized it wouldn't be easy to gain an admission. There were only twenty-four seats, and applications came in by the thousands. The applicant had to go through the selection process of written exam, group discussion and an interview with three members of the faculty.

I reached the last step, the interview. The day of the interview, I saw many sharply dressed applicants waiting for their turn. The serious faces of students leaving after the interview added to the nervousness I already felt.

When it was my turn, I entered, greeted them and sat down on the one chair placed across an impressive heavy desk. On the other side, seated, were two well-dressed male professors. By the window, with her feet up on the sill, sat a woman on a chair. She didn't look as professional, with her chiffon sari falling all over the place, often exposing her chest. Her hair looked tousled.

The male interviewers, dressed in suits, reflected the seriousness of their task. They took turns asking questions, their faces blank and unfriendly. I was able to answer them with reasonable ease. As they progressed with questions requiring some thought to answer, the lady interviewer laughed loudly, as if she found my answers stupid. Though distracted, I stayed focused on the question. Again, she laughed. After the third distraction, I stopped talking.

"Excuse me, Sir. I'll finish my answer, but before that, I want to ask this lady why she is laughing at me."

I was admitted to the MBA program. I concluded having one interviewer disturb the state of mind of an interviewee was in itself a test to observe the reactions of the candidate, a strategy for elimination. The less confident may lose attention and not stay focused on the question. The way I responded to the situation must have impressed them.

I was concerned about the tuition; I didn't like that my Dad would have added expenses. But, Dad told me not to worry about it. Luckily, I didn't have to feel burdensome for long. A rich textile mill owner wanting to encourage formal education in business management announced an award for the student with the highest score in undergraduate commerce education. I received enough money to cover my first year's tuition, and a gold medal. During the summer vacation, the program placed students at various businesses for paid internships. That income covered the tuition for the second year.

The curriculum was intense. School started early in the morning. I couldn't help Mom with housework. That bothered me. Motabhai and Bhabhi barely had enough time to have lunch that she cooked, before going to work. Mom didn't have much help in the household chores. But, she managed. She even made fresh *rotis* when I came home around one p.m., for lunch. Then, I'd bike back to school and she'd get to rest a little.

In August of 1978, our extended family, on my mom's side, suffered a devastating loss. My aunt Savita died at a very young age. She had a hysterectomy, but some complications developed and the doctors couldn't save her. Aunt Savita was my Hasmukh mama's wife. She left behind three young children— son, Urvish was sixteen, daughter, Harsha was thirteen, and the youngest son, Dhruv, was only nine.

It was a sad repetition of my mother's childhood. When my maternal grandmother died at the age of 40, she left behind six children. Mother was the oldest, followed by two sisters and three brothers. My Hasmukh mama was only twelve.

My mother and Hasmukh mama had a special bond. I remember him coming to our home in Chandra Colony, on Sundays. He sat in the kitchen on a chair behind the door and the two talked, while Mom continued with her chores. They shared their problems and challenges with each other. He didn't like to see my mother feeling sad. They took care of each other. Mama loved and admired my father, as well. He brought so much joy to all around him. Hasmukh would bring candies called Gems, round, chocolate candies with a hard shell.

When Aunt Savita passed away, Mom brought Dhruv home to live with us. He was a cute little boy, with a curious face. My dad enrolled him in a Gujarati medium school, located in walking distance from our home. I helped him with schoolwork. But, it was easy to see he was sad and lost.

Mayank progressed in the banking industry. His math skills made his work with numbers easy to master.

Bhabhi was adjusting to our family. We had no choice but

to help her integrate with us. She was the youngest of the seven children in her dad's family, and, therefore, wasn't trained in household chores. The biggest problem my mom had with Disha was that she wasn't as clean as her. Another issue was she didn't know English and felt out of place when we were among Motabhai and Dad's professional friends.

But Disha had what we did not. The ability to cleverly avoid responsibility, the way of talking that got her out of any tough situation and yet have people adore her. We spoke what we thought and expected the world to acknowledge us for our generosity and honesty. She never meant what she said. She was street smart. We began to see the advantage of having her among us. If someone asked to visit, she made him or her feel welcome while canceling the visit. If a surprise guest was angling for dinner, she got rid of them without offering even a cup of tea. Family and friends alike adored her. Her uncanny ability to refuse to do something without actually saying "no" was very impressive. We started taking advantage of her personality traits for situations where we felt awkward. If we were worried about damaging a relationship, she'd take over without a hint and make it even stronger. She became an asset.

Mom took her under her wings and trained her in housework and in living conservatively. Bhabhi was from a rich family but she didn't seem to mind our constant shortage of money.

CHAPTER ELEVEN

1980-81: PART 1

I started working right after graduation. In 1980 the idea of a professionally trained woman occupying a management or a decision-making position was so new, one of the newspapers decided to write about it. They interviewed me and one other graduate. We were featured in the newspaper, with photographs. My dad, who read every word of three newspapers every day, was so thrilled that morning. He sat down with a pair of scissors and clipped out the article.

I was hired by Gujarat State Financial Corporation engaged in funding small scale manufacturing start-ups. At the age of twenty-two I was an Assistant Marketing Manager with a staff of forty-seven, all of them much older than me. I went to work dressed in my *Salwar-kameez,* a long top with leggings and a long chiffon scarf going from one shoulder to the other in the front. It was what I wore all the time before I started working.

In a few weeks of working there it occurred to me although the staff was friendly, they were not always providing me with the help I needed. They thought of me as a friend, not as a superior. Some of the questions and comments were related to my age, which made me realize they were not able to accept me as their boss because I looked too young.

I changed the way I dressed. I started wearing sarees to work. It made me look mature. When I left home and came down the stairs, dressed in cotton sarees, crisp with starch and carefully ironed, all the ladies in the neighborhood came out of their kitchens to have a look at me. "Arunaben, she's leaving." One of them would sound an alarm for the others to come out. They were impressed with me and encouraged their young daughters to be like me. "Aww, look how nice she looks, with that cotton saree. And that long thick braid going down. She has no make-up on and yet she looks so elegant, like Indira Gandhi." I was embarrassed to say the least, but I could see my mother's chest rising with pride.

My friendly ways of making people feel comfortable helped in making the staff accept me. Pretty soon some one or the other from the team would show up in my cabin asking me about the type of data they needed to find for me. One older staff member, probably older than my dad, started thinking of me as a daughter he wished he had and even watched out for me.

I was doing market research for various industries to assess the demand for their product or products. If there were enough factories manufacturing a particular kind of product/s then the corporation would know not to advance funds to applicants wanting to manufacture similar products; this ensured the success of the ones already in operations and prevented potential failures of the new start-ups.

Based on the number of applications for manufacturing a particular item, the board of directors requested a study of that industry. I researched the data of the existing clients and contacted each one of them for more information about their production data, sales, availability of raw materials and other operational details.

After analyzing the data, I selected a few companies to visit to interview the top officials, accountants, and marketing staff. The actual visits and conversations at the sites helped me arrive at conclusions and make recommendations to the marketing director about the viability of new manufacturing plants.

Most of these factories would be located far from the city, in designated industrial parks. To get there, I would have to use public transportation or borrow my dad's Vespa. My dad worried about me; a young girl going to remote areas, visiting places where there would be few or no women. Sometimes, he would take a day off and go with me. We were a team, my dad and me.

With a lot of enthusiasm and pride I prepared reports for the board of directors. After all, my observations and conclusions had the potential to affect the manufacturing environment of the state. The future of many people depended on what I presented, so I understood the importance of what I was doing.

I submitted my reports to the marketing director who would then present them to the board at the monthly meeting. However, the report I submitted wouldn't always be the report the Directors got to read. Rampant and systemic corruption played its role. Who the loan applicant was or how much percentage of the loan the applicant offered to the officials with power and position, affected their decisions.

My reports began to feel like exercises in futility, I was discouraged. Sometimes I called up the CEO on his private line to complain about my boss. He assured me he would look into it and reminded me the phone line was for special purpose and not for complaining about other staff members.

School equipped me with the tools to do my job well. Observing dad at work, taught me a strong work ethic and value of hard work. But nothing had prepared me for the real world. At the young age of 22, I thought I could change the world; the world I had not yet seen. I was depressed. Sometimes I did not want to go to work.

CHAPTER TWELVE
1980-81: PART 2

In early 1981, after prolonged illness due to a weak heart and asthma, my paternal grandmother who lived with us, passed away. We took care of her until the end. Again, the family finances suffered. Grandmother's medications, doctor's home visits, the tea and food expenses for the constant flow of relatives coming to see her took a toll on our purses. After her passing, we were obligated to hold the thirteen-day posthumous ceremonies and dinners. That only made matters worse.

When grandma died, Dad's sister in England, with whom my brother Suresh lived, came for the ceremonies. She asked Dad for the money he owed for keeping Suresh. While Dad was thankful for what she did for Suresh's future, he was in no position to give her the Rs. 20,000 she asked for.

Dad became ill. He started vomiting and his blood pressure went up. From the past episodes I could tell he was reacting to stress about money. I knew the pattern. I asked mother why he was sick, since we had already figured out a way to pay for the recent added expenses.

"Manufoi wants to be paid for Suresh's expenses."

As usual, I reacted strongly, "What? Now? How much? Her Mom just died; how could she think about that?" I was angry at my aunt for not being thoughtful and grateful for what my parents had done for her parents. But, then I offered Dad Rs. 13000 I saved from my monthly income. Motabhai also helped. Dad didn't like to take my money but the need to pay my aunt took precedence.

Later in July of 1981, Bhabhi gave birth to a baby boy.

My parents were happy beyond belief. Despite the tradition of the daughter-in-law staying at her parents' home for a month and a half after childbirth, Mom brought Bhabhi to our home. She made herbal, medicinal foods for her so her body recovered from the trauma of childbirth. A special lady came to our home to give oil massages to the baby and exercise his little arms and legs. The lady gave him a bath every day, before she left.

Life changed for all of us.

Bhabhi changed. She became more assertive. Someone who was always ready to please Mom, she showed signs of defiance. We noticed she believed in the old orthodox ideas of the superiority of the male gender. If she felt any inadequacies before, they disappeared completely. She had given birth to a boy, a male heir to the family.

Mom and Dad were in love with their first grandson. Mom was too busy with running the home and didn't have time to express her joy. But Dad's time at home revolved around Keval. It felt as if Dad's mother's soul came back in the form of Dad's grandson.

CHAPTER THIRTEEN

1980-81: PART 3

When Bhabhi went back to work, life became harder for my Mom. They returned to the previous arrangement of living at the flat. Coming to Chandra Colony before going to work got even later. Like a tornado they'd come with their son, rush through lunch Mom prepared and run out the door to go to work.

Mom was left to clean up after lunch, finish laundry and take care of Keval all day long. In the past, Bhabhi used to buy fresh vegetables for the next day's lunch, because her work was close to the main vegetable market in the old city of Ahmedabad. We'd then sit together to clean and chop the vegetables. In winter, there were many more varieties of vegetables available to us. All of my favorite green leafy vegetables grew in winter. The large leaves of *tandaljo* (*amaranthus*) were easy to chop. But, the fresh green garlic had a strong smell, so we let Mom chop it. She was an avid reader of health information in the newspapers and learned garlic was good for hypertension. She sautéed it in *ghee* and filled up a container, so Dad could have a spoonful every day.

After Keval's birth, Bhabhi stopped getting the vegetables.

She did not want to waste time and delay coming home to be with her son. I felt torn between my job and Mom's plight.

At work, I felt frustrated and agitated.

Dad advised me to follow the rules, not make waves, and do my part. He said, "You do your job and be happy you did it well. Leave the rest alone, you can't change the system."

"I can't change the system, but I can quit." I countered.

"Ili, you have a tendency to get carried away by your feelings. Don't get emotional. This is a good job for a girl. There is no stress; you are getting a good salary and benefits. Government jobs are good. In the private industry they make you work hard."

He advised me to look at the positives of a government job- the benefits, the pension, and the choice of not having to work too hard and therefore, stress free.

I was angry with the government and the adults who were destroying the country in order to fill their pockets. Dad's words made me feel lost, because my urge to find a more fulfilling job would not go away.

But, Mom also encouraged me to be less intense and more carefree. She enjoyed the subsidized groceries from the government. Oftentimes, the factories my company financed sold their products to the employees at a discount. Our family acquired its first blender because of my job. My mother did not mind such benefits.

CHAPTER FOURTEEN
1981-82: PART 1

Not knowing what I could do initially, I found ways of staying busy at work. I had two friends in the accounting department, Gala, a CPA, and Charu, a clerk. Gala, though highly educated and in a high position, was not allotted a personal office, but I had a nice big private space to myself.

I liked having my own office. It was large. My desk sat facing the entrance. Behind me, was a wall with large windows. The windows looked into the courtyard, making my room well lit. When it was not hot, I kept them open for fresh air.

I invited Gala and Charu to my office for tea. The corporation maintained a kitchen where an employee made fresh tea every time an officer requested it. The three of us enjoyed our tea meetings.

I often wondered if I should start a business. I remembered how the members of SEWA, Ela Bhatt's trade union, helped uneducated, poor women. When Mom bought big sacks of seasonal grains, we had to spend hours and hours sifting through them to remove rocks and dirt escaped the farmers' attention. It was boring work. I hated it. I was sure, women and their daughters everywhere, also hated the tedious process. Perhaps, some of those women from SEWA could sift through the grains and legumes. I could hire them to do the work, then package the grains and legumes into smaller packaging and sell them. I was certain women in every household would appreciate this service.

After a while, the excitement of tea parties subsided. Sitting alone in my office it occurred to me, essentially, I had no supervisor. I could leave the office anytime and stay out as long as I wanted. No one questioned my absence. They assumed I was out researching.

I took advantage of my situation of my situation and started looking for a different job. Scanning the classified section of the newspaper in my office, I talked with the human resources manager at the companies looking to hire, I made limited trips for interviews to the jobs that appealed to me.

Once, I visited Shilpi Ad Agency, the second largest advertising agency in India. I was hoping to get a job as an advertising agent or an account representative. I walked in and talked to the branch manager. "Do you have any job vacancies?"

"No, we don't." He said, "Currently, we are not looking to fill any positions."

Disappointed, as I turned to walk away, I paused and asked another question, "What is your interview process?"

"We have the interviewee do a case study, you know, we ask you to create an ad for a new product, or plan a comprehensive ad campaign for our client. The response goes to the main office in Bombay. If the hiring department is satisfied with the candidate's submission, we call them for an interview. After, we send out an appointment letter.

I took a chance and asked, "Can I attempt the first step, the case study? You can send my report to Bombay or keep it in your file. When there is an opening, you can evaluate it and consider me."

After some hesitation, the branch manager agreed. He asked me to design a print ad to introduce a new detergent. Methodically, I listed the detergents currently available in the market and the attributes the manufacturers emphasized in their advertisements. I tried to remember conversations Mom had with neighbors and relatives about why she bought the detergent we used. I searched for something about detergents that was important, and yet wasn't emphasized by the existing detergent manufacturers. Once, I found one specific quality missing in current ads, I designed the ad for the new detergent. Pleased with what I was able to do, but unsure of ever hearing from them, I turned it in and left.

CHAPTER FIFTEEN
1981-82: PART 2

Despite the turmoil my job caused me, it was the first time our family had some disposable income, and that made me proud and happy.

In India, children did not move out of their home after they started earning an income. The boys would live in the same home with their parents, even after they were married. On the other hand a girl, whether she worked or not, would move out of the father's home only to move into the husband's or rather the father-in-law's home, after marriage.

All of my salary was extra income for the family. Growing up in a lower middle class family taught me to be thrifty. My spending habits were conservative. The fear of not having enough money was so strong I understood the difference between a need and a want, quite well. I saved my entire paycheck. This allowed my mother and I to splurge a little, now and then.

At times, I came home from work to a hot cup of tea and my mother dressed up and ready to go out. It was obvious I had to finish my tea quickly so we could leave to go for a walk around the Law Garden, or to an exhibition sale of *Sarees*.

My mother was a very curious woman. Oftentimes, if she found out from a friend or from the newspaper a psychic or a famous astrologer was in town, she wanted to go and check him out for herself. Dad did not always cooperate with her, so I ended up going on those adventures with her.

One day, she wanted to revisit a Seer she had gone to meet once before, with her friend. She asked me to drive her there, on the Vespa. Dad was happy to be relieved of such obligations, so he didn't mind when I used his scooter for our rendezvous. Once we reached the approximate area, very far out of town, I asked her to notify me when we were at the building. But there was no building to be found.

"It was right here," she exclaimed righteously. She had absolutely no sense of direction.

"Mom, how can a whole building disappear in a few days?" I teased her. Needless to say, we had to turn back and go home.

CHAPTER SIXTEEN

1982: PART 1

Walking back from work I looked forward to having a hot cup of chai, with Mom. I was curious to find out what she had planned for our evening.

My workplace was about three miles away from home. Sometimes, I would walk. Other times I would catch a rickshaw, a black and yellow three–wheeler.

Often Dad took a detour from his work to pick me up and we would go home together.

That day I decided to walk.

I liked walking. On the way, I passed a park, Law Garden, named for its location across from a School of Law. This garden, as parks are called in India, played a big part in my childhood. When my brother and I, along with the two sons of our landlord were in our early teens, Dad used to get us up early in the morning and drag us out to the park for a morning walk. We all hated it. As a reward for going with him he'd buy us a bottle of flavored milk from a little shop near the park. We loved that. My favorite flavor was pistachio.

There was a *Shiva* temple on the way home. The temple

became busy about the time I passed by because it was time for *Aarti*. Performed at temples in the morning and in the evening, *Aarti* is a ritualistic prayer during which the priest holds a silver plate with a light, made of cotton and *ghee*, on it and moves it in vertical motion, illuminating the statue of the Deity. People in attendance chant prayers. One of the helpers moves his hand in a vertical motion with a brass bell and another on huge drums, providing rhythm for the prayers. The rest of the attendees clap their hands while singing the prayers. The *Aarti* is meant to remind us of the greatness of God because the flame we rotate is symbolic of the Cosmos (Sun, Moon, Stars) revolving around the Almighty, paying respect. People often stop at the temple and participate in the ritual of Aarti. The air is filled with fragrance from the sandalwood incense burning in the temple. The atmosphere is unique, calm amidst the chaos. The feeling transcends all the ideas or beliefs I've had, about God.

When I reached home, after the Aarti, Mom had the chai ready. However, I got a strange feeling. My parents were in an unusual mood. Dad, who I usually found sitting in an easy chair reading the newspaper, was also dressed and ready to leave. *To go where?* I couldn't tell.

"Why did you walk?" she asked.

Confused, I asked, "Why not?"

"Uncle Satish has brought a proposal for your marriage. We have to go to the boy's house this evening to meet him and the family."

"What?" I did not expect that answer. "I thought Dad was going to wait until I was ready."

"Yes. But this is too good an opportunity to pass up. Freshen up, wear this pretty *saree* and put on this gold jewelry. You have to look attractive."

I was still recovering from the bombshell that had just dropped. Betrayal is too harsh a description of how I felt, but the suddenness had knocked the wind out of me. I could barely breathe.

"Why?"

Mom was totally in the moment, unaware of what I was thinking or feeling. She went on, "Because you have to look good so they have a favorable first impression. It's a very good family from a very high social status. We are lucky they agreed to consider you. They have already screened many young girls. The boy lives in America."

Although the whole situation, I was suddenly thrown into, took me by surprise, Mom's last statement did not surprise me at all.

Even during the time in which Dad had promised he would not talk about my marriage, many times he had tried to, gently, introduce the subject. Most of the time it was when he heard about an eligible bachelor from America. But, I kept discouraging him because I did not want to leave India. I loved the life I was living and I had plans for my future. I aspired to work, save a lot of money and start my business in the same concept as the SEWA organization. My dad, on the other hand, was determined to send all three of his children to America.

"What do you mean, we are lucky to be considered." Now I was getting angry and annoyed.

Mom was adamant. She tried to convince me we had arrived at a golden opportunity, one we could not have imagined.

"We are an ordinary, middle class family. They are famous, very high in society, and very well to do." I could hear the desperation in her voice.

Apparently, Gautam's grandfather was a prominent

attorney. He had worked with Gandhi and other leaders of Indian National Congress, against the British, during India's freedom movement. After independence, he started his law practice and his success had been so great he was able to purchase many parcels of land all over the city of Ahmedabad.

Gautam's father was also a practicing lawyer, before he emmigrated to the USA with his family. The entire family was in California, except for the one uncle at whose house we were going to meet Gautam and his parents. Gautam was in New York learning to be a general surgeon. Gautam's family belonged to the Brahmin caste, which was very important to my family. My parents could hardly contain their excitement.

Uncle Satish was friends with the Gautam's uncle, and found out from him Gautam and his parents were in Ahmedabad for the sole purpose of arranging his marriage.

My uncle and I had a special bond. He was amused by my bold and progressive opinions, especially about equality for women, and my fearlessness to take on causes for the fair treatment of women. We enjoyed having long and interesting discussions on many such topics. He called me, "Jhansi Ki Rani." Laxmibai, queen of the province of Jhansi in North India was an impressive figure in Indian history. She fought bravely against the British occupation of India, sometimes as a ruler and sometimes in disguise, until she was killed in the battle in 1858, ninety-nine years before India became independent. She became a symbol of resistance to British rule, for the Indian nationalists.

My parents wanted this arrangement to work so desperately they were looking for signs of a good omen. "Uncle Satish brought this proposal for you. This arrangement will work because you are special to him." Mom expressed her hope.

Giving up, I said, "I don't want to dress up. Let's go."

Mom insisted, "You have to dress up. You need to look presentable and attractive."

I never liked the idea of a girl having to dress up and look her best for such a gathering. "Why do I have to dress up? That would be the fake me. I don't look like that all the time. "

The potential groom wears what he always wears in his regular life. There is no formal dress for him, so he can go straight from work to meet a potential bride, but a girl has to make herself presentable.

And then, there is the issue of being selected for one's looks rather than for the person one is. What happens to the girls who are not pretty or whose parents can't afford nice clothing or jewelry? Do they have to get married into a family that is just as poor and as unimportant as theirs?

A girl of marriageable age would have to dress up and experience the uncomfortable process many times before a family found her acceptable.

There is a wide range of ways a marriage was arranged then. There are situations where parents have agreed their kids will be married when they grow up. Then, there is the kind of arrangement where the two young people meet when the families come together, and the two get a glimpse of each other, not just visually but also philosophically, because of the conversations that go on between the families. If the values and ideologies of the two families are compatible, it is safe to assume the children of the two families would also be compatible in their own beliefs and opinions on important matters of life. The broader, more liberal, version of an arranged marriage, allows the two to meet privately, after the families have met, so they can talk with each other uninterrupted, and get to learn more about each other's dreams, values, opinions, likes and dislikes.

I did not change my saree or put on makeup. All of us, my

parents, Motabhai, Disha and their infant son and I, left for Gautam's uncle's home, where he and his parents were staying.

During the rickshaw ride, I was confused because I did not understand what I was supposed to feel. Should I be excited? Where is the excitement in having to leave your own family and go live among strangers? And these strangers live in America; so far away from everyone I know and love.

We reached their house but I was so engrossed in my thoughts, I didn't even notice getting there.

Their house stood well above ground and had a large, covered patio, which could be accessed by wide impressive steps on both sides. The size itself was enough to impress anyone. We had never seen a house like that before. It reminded me of the royal palaces in the old days.

We entered their living room, which was a large rectangular room with a heavy solid wood entrance door, and another door on the wall across, dividing the room in halves. There were bookcases all along the walls. Chairs were lined in front of them to accommodate everyone.

By the time we entered the house all the other parties involved in this process were already there, occupying all but a few chairs; Uncle Satish and his wife, Auntie Alka, the potential groom and his parents, his uncle and his family, and the grandmother, all of them waiting for us.

I felt awkward, everyone's eyes were on me, as we entered. I was not happy.

His father welcomed us and gestured to us to have a seat. Once we sat down, and everyone introduced, conversations began. Most of the talking was happening between Uncle Satish and Gautam's father. It was as if they were in a competition to see who could dominate the scene. Uncle bragged about me, listed all my qualifications: MBA, fluent in English, working in middle management at a reputed Government Financial Corporation, well-read, caring, and respectful of elderly, speaks her mind, and most of all, honest to a fault.

His dad was not the one to accept defeat. He went on and on about his son. A general surgeon, went to New York all by himself, independent thinker, got accepted in a residency program ten days after landing at John F Kennedy airport, saved his grandfather's life twice when he walked in on his grandfather suffering a heart attack.

Mr. Pandit, Gautam's father, also went on and on about the grand past of the family. Grandfather's trip to the prison during freedom movement, his successful law practice after independence, owned a lot of land, designed the house we were sitting in, fashioned after the palaces in Rajasthan, so on and so forth.

Gautam's mother, uncle, and grandmother, tried to make him stop from monopolizing the conversation, but he ignored them.

I was bored. I tried to look up a couple of times during the evening to get a glance at Gautam, who was sitting in one corner wearing a white shirt and jeans. He seemed decent looking. I saw him trying to take a good look at me. It was hard to tell if he thought I was good looking. I didn't care. It was getting late.

My parents, like many Indians, had a deep faith in astrology. A large number of marriages are arranged after making sure the girl's and boy's horoscopes match. When my dad found an opening in the conversation, he asked, "Do you believe in matching the horoscopes?"

Mr. and Mrs. Pandit did not sound too worried about matching the horoscopes but they were respectful of my dad's faith in them.

At last, the evening ended with the adults of the family deciding my dad would be going to his trusted astrologer with our horoscopes. If the horoscopes matched, proving our stars were compatible Gautam and I would be allowed to meet privately.

CHAPTER SEVENTEEN

1982: PART 2

The following day, my parents couldn't wait to go to my dad's maternal uncle for getting the horoscopes read, the only thing in their way of my marriage to Gautam. Sometimes, even if the horoscopes didn't match perfectly, as long as the set of stars of the two people don't clash in their houses or positions, reckoning of some very negative future events, it would be considered acceptable. My parents wanted to make sure my future was reasonably safe from extremely unfortunate events due to the non-compatible stars.

My father went to visit his uncle, who was a very reliable astrologer. Uncle looked at the horoscopes and the charts reflecting positions of the moon, sun, Jupiter, Mercury, and Venus in both horoscopes. He superimposed the charts and did calculations based on the degrees of the stars' locations, at the birth times of both of us, to make sure they were not in conflict, and concluded our horoscopes matched.

Uncle exclaimed with delight, "The degree to which their stars match is very high, together they'll make a powerful couple. I approve." He had uttered the words my dad wanted to hear.

Happiness dripped from his face as he entered home that evening. "Let's see if Ela and Gautam can meet today, so they can decide if they like each other."

The next day, after work, my brother, sister-in-law and I went to Gautam's uncle's house so Gautam and I could meet privately. I did not dress up. I wore *salwar-kameez,* a long top and pants with a scarf, something I was more comfortable wearing. My long thick hair hung in one braid, reaching my lower back.

When we arrived, Gautam's uncle's young children, daughter in her early teens and son about eight years old, stood curiously by the door. After a few formal greetings, Gautam was instructed to escort me to a room on the second floor.

His complexion was fairer compared to most Gujarati men, and he was taller than most Gujarati men. His height was an important consideration for us. At five feet six inches I was taller than most Gujarati girls, and my parents worried about being able to find a husband taller than me. He was dressed comfortably- jeans and a T-shirt, and flip-flops on his feet, a common tradition among people with larger houses. Perhaps because big houses cannot be swept and mopped as frequently as smaller homes, like ours.

The house was even more impressive than had seemed before. The living room opened into a courtyard with walls on four sides and open to the sky. It was square with each side between twenty to thirty feet long. On the front part of the house, in the middle was the living room, where we met before. On both sides of the living room was a bedroom. The living room opened into the courtyard, to the right of which was a wooden staircase, tucked away in the corner. We had to climb a set of two staircases to get to the second floor. The stairs ended in a wraparound balcony about eight to ten feet wide looking down into the courtyard.

We entered a large sitting room, sitting just above the living room below. Again, there were bedrooms on both sides; the three rooms formed one side of the square. We settled down across from each other on the sofa set placed in one corner of the room.

This was a new experience for me. Usually bold and unafraid to talk with strangers, I had never spoken with someone with the explicit purpose of screening him for a potential husband. I was told his father had arranged for him to meet many young ladies, I was the last one they had added due to Uncle Satish's request. The only thought in my mind was, "Did he not like any one of them, or did they not approve of him?"

"Do you have anything you want to know about me?" He started the conversation as soon as we sat down.

Just then I realized I should have taken this situation more seriously. I fumbled. Then words just came out of my mouth. "Do you smoke?"

"No I don't smoke," he answered. He sounded believable.

"Do you drink alcohol?" My Brahmin upbringing came to my rescue as I struggled to find things to talk about. It is believed Brahmins are the caste of people closest to God. They are the descendants of the gurus who studied the Vedas and passed on the knowledge through generations. Traditionally, no Brahmin would smoke, drink or eat meat. Or so it is believed. But still, asking him gave me time to think.

"Will you mind if I work? I would like to have a career." With relief, I was able to ask about something very important to me. "I am educated and would hate for it to go to waste."

"I have no problem with you pursuing a career or even more education. My grandfather and his friends used to kidnap young girls who were being forced into marriage with older men. The girls were put in a care-home and offered education. He was a social reformer." He spoke with pride. "My mother went to school after she was married to my dad."

I was impressed. His grandfather seemed like someone I would have enjoyed meeting. My strong feelings about equality for women resonated with his grandfather's ideology and actions.

I was analyzing the situation. Because of my dad's determination, almost obsession, with sending me to America, I knew if I didn't accept Gautam, Dad would find someone else who'd be from America.

I knew I was one of the very few in our Brahmin sub-community who could converse in English and had a professional education, so it was going to be difficult to find an equally educated match for me. Gautam was highly educated.

I also knew my ideas of gender equality were uncommon at the time, making it difficult for me to fit in easily with any family. Gautam's grandfather and the culture he had promoted in his family matched my personal philosophy.

Everyone knew any young man or woman who came to India with a mission to find a bride or a groom did not have much time to allow for multiple meetings to get to know each other or fall in love. Love had to come after marriage.

If the basic concerns were eliminated, I knew I could create a life I wanted for myself. I was not going to find a better family to marry into.

Still, I did not like the whole situation of arranged to be married, and having to leave India. At best it was a compromise.

When I snapped out of my thoughts, I asked him, "Do you have any questions for me?"

"My work days are long. Sometimes I have to stay at the

hospital overnight. Will you be able to handle that?" He asked me.

I did not understand the point of his question. If one has to do a good job one must do what is necessary. Why did he ask such a question? "I will be fine by myself." I spoke with confidence. "You will be busy with your work and once I am settled I will also be busy with my own job."

He continued to inform me about his life in New York and his passion for surgery. He described how he almost walked away from an interview when the director of a surgery residency program suggested he accept a residency in internal medicine for one year, before transferring to residency in surgery.

"I told the director if I can't be a surgeon I don't want to be a doctor, I would wait. That's when he allowed me into the program even though I was one month late." He was proud of his passion and determination.

We talked for what felt like an hour or less. We decided we'd inform our parents of our decision and went downstairs to where my brother and sister-in-law were waiting. I noticed Gautam's father was entertaining them with his monologues, over a cup of chai.

We arrived home to my anxious mother, buzzing with questions. "How did it go? Do you like him? Do you think he will agree to marry you?" The questions from her kept coming at me as if her life depended on my answers.

"I don't know." I didn't know what to tell her. I didn't know how to behave in this situation. I was certainly not excited about it. But most of all, I did not like how desperate my mother acted.

"We will see what he says." I replied without enthusiasm.

My parents waited impatiently to hear from Gautam's family. We did not hear from them. Nobody came by. There was no news. Mom was emotional, "We are not well known and rich. Why would a family like theirs want our daughter in their family?"

My parents believed despite their limited resources they had gone above and beyond in their efforts, to raise me to become a highly eligible young lady. I had felt their strong need to see me intellectually and educationally attractive to the parents coming from abroad for their son's marriage.

My perception of their desires, my keen sense of responsibility towards them, as well as my need to make them happy and proud, motivated me to work hard in school and stay focused. I turned out to be more than what they had expected. I could sense pride in them.

When Gautam's parents did not rush to our humble home, with the decision to accept me for their son, my parents felt sad and disappointed.

Whether their disappointment was because they felt their lower socio-economic position was in my way of a better life or they had lost a perfect opportunity to fulfill their dreams of going to America, I couldn't tell.

CHAPTER EIGHTEEN

1982: PART 3

It had been two days since Gautam and I met privately for the first time. I was busy helping my mother with the morning chores, sweeping and mopping the floors, and hanging the washed clothes on the line.

Mornings were always hectic. Short of time, I pushed myself every morning to finish as many chores as possible so Mom didn't have to do them after we left for work. She had to look after my brother's infant son and my grandfather.

I was in the middle of hanging clothes on the line in the compound of the rental property, when I saw Gautam's father walk in from the gate. He asked me if my dad was home. I told him we lived upstairs on the second floor. I kept hanging the clothes as I watched him climb up the steep, narrow stairs and enter our home.

When I went up to the house after finishing my work, I saw my dad talking with Gautam's father. None of them wanted to speak with me or ask me anything, which was just fine by me. I kept on doing what I did every morning. After about half an hour Gautam's dad left. The whole visit seemed strange to me.

Since I was trying to avoid the unavoidable I did not bother to ask Dad about it.

Next morning, he showed up again. I was annoyed to see him. Why was he coming? I didn't like someone in our small living room, when I was sweeping and mopping the floor. Did he not know he was in the way? Who visits in the morning during the hustle and bustle of the day?

But it was different today. He wanted to talk with me. He addressed me with a question while I was helping my grandfather. I requested him to wait until I was done, hoping he would not be offended. He was not. Darn, I thought to myself.

"Elaben, one must learn to recognize an opportunity when one comes their way," he told me. "Why are you not interested in my son?"

I was surprised by his question.

"Well, I don't know your son very well," I told him honestly.

"Besides, my younger brother is in the UK. I am not sure he will be able to come for the wedding. I would prefer if we got engaged now, but we wait for the wedding, so we can plan for my brother to attend." I suggested hoping if he agreed Gautam and I would get time to know each other.

As I was speaking I was watching my parents' faces. Mom's showed relief, her daughter was not rejected after all. Dad seemed pleased as well. Both of them were too happy to pay attention to what I was saying.

"Well, my son has met many eligible young ladies during this visit. But he was not sure about any of them. Now he has informed me if you do not agree to marry him, he is ready to go back to the USA." He continued, "It is not easy for him to take time off to come to India frequently. We would like to see him married during this visit. Please think about it."

He was eager to get his son married. He promised, "You know, once you come to America, Gautam will make sure you go to England and see your brother."

"This is such a nice family, Ela. Babubhai is a gentleman. He addressed your concern about not having Suresh here. Isn't that nice?" Dad was trying to convince me to agree for marriage.

Mom chimed in, "At first I was worried about sending you far from us, with no one there to help you. But now I know Gautam has his parents, two brothers, two uncles, an aunt and many cousins in America. You will not be lonely. The family members will take care of you."

"Horoscopes match, Gautam is educated, tall, and handsome. The family is Brahmin, and there are a lot of family members in America to take care of you. We could not find a better match than this," Dad continued.

It was decided. I would marry Gautam.

Our formal engagement was on February 14, 1982, eight days after we had first laid eyes on each other. It was held at Gautam's uncle's house.

Later, I learned his parents did not have a home in India. My relatives—Dad's siblings, Mom's siblings, Dad and Mom's uncles and aunts, cousins, and my cousins all attended the engagement ceremony. The house, a reflection of the prosperity of my new family, impressed them. My parents were proud of having found a perfect family for their daughter.

My cousins were impressed for one more reason. My cousin sisters thought Gautam looked like Dev Anand, a popular Indian actor.

The wedding was set for February 20, fourteen days after we first met.

CHAPTER NINETEEN

1982: PART 4

There were only six days to prepare for the wedding. To say things got busy would be an understatement.

Both sets of parents had to meet and sort out the procedural matters. Cultural norms dictate many of those, making it easier to negotiate. The bride's parents would host the wedding ceremony, and luncheon or dinner, based on the time of the wedding.

The groom's parents would host the reception.

An Indian wedding is an elaborate affair based on religious and spiritual beliefs and practices. The astrologer or the priest determines the most auspicious time when the priest puts the bride's hand into the hand of the groom. The ceremony is known as *Hasta Melap*. All other events and ceremonies had to be arranged around one specific time. Our *Hasta Melap* had to be in the early evening.

The first order of business was the printing of the invitation cards. Once the timeline was established both families got their own cards printed. On the 19th, both families had *Gruh Shanti* , at their respective homes. It is a ceremony inviting all the Gods and the planets to bless the house and the family. On the 20th, my parents arranged for a luncheon at the venue of the wedding, Punjabi Hall, where all the relatives and friends of my family were invited. My parents invited close relatives of Gautam's family. The wedding was in the evening, followed by dinner. On the 21st, Gautam's family hosted a luncheon where close family members and friends of both sides were invited. Reception was at the Orient Club in the evening.

The bride's parents are supposed to gift their daughter a certain number of outfits, mostly sarees. This meant we had to go shopping for at least eleven sarees, get the blouses stitched, and get matching petticoats. I didn't have time to shop for these sarees, my best friend and my sister-in-law accomplished this task.

As per tradition, Gautam's family had to give me two sarees, one of them I'd wear at the reception. His mom, aunt (wife of the uncle at whose house they were staying), and I went shopping for the sarees. My mother-in-law picked bright colored sarees. I chose a cream-colored silk saree with a wide deep red border and a dark navy blue one with small silver round patterns strewn all over the six yards and bright red border and *pallu* with beautiful silver and navy blue intricate rich pattern. *Pallu* is the part of saree that shows in the front when it is worn in Gujarati style. Gautam's mother thought my taste in sarees was like that of old women.

The bride's family also gifted her gold jewelry. In the old days, when girls were not allowed education, gold was the only thing of value they owned. It was a form of insurance parents bought just in case her husband suffered poor health or died prematurely. The tradition continues to this day. I am not sure why the groom's family gives gold to the daughter-in-law.

Gautam and I were leaving his house to spend some time together when his mom wanted me to go with her to the goldsmith, to select the gold jewelry they wanted to give me. We went to a goldsmith in the old city. The sets they showed me were too big and imposing. I wondered where I'd wear something like that, in America. Gautam's mother informed me her budget was to give me ten *tola*, 100 grams of gold. Within that limit, I was free to choose whatever I liked. I decided to get two less heavy sets.

Although everyone in my family was excited, I was not. I was worried about the financial burden my wedding was causing my dad. It had not been a year since my grandmother passed away and father had to pay for all the posthumous ceremonies and dinners for thirteen days. Our family had spent money on the medical care for Grandma when she was very ill, just before she passed away. During the last year, we also had increased expenses for the new member of our family, my nephew Keval.

I knew my parents did not have money to pay for the wedding. They'd have to borrow money against Mom's gold jewelry. That bothered me.

On the morning of the wedding, at the family luncheon, I wore a brown silk saree with black border. Motabhai and Disha bought it for me during their trip to South India. Gautam came with his family. We had lunch together, but it was awkward. Neither one of us knew how to behave with each other, especially around so many people. On top of everything else, Gautam was not feeling well. He had a fever.

I got ready for the wedding at home. My friend, Sonal, did my hair. She tried to put my hair up in a bun, but my hair was too heavy and soft. We ended up with some kind of simple hairstyle. She had bought a few items of make-up. This included my first lipstick, which she applied on me.

Traditionally the wedding outfit, *panetar,* a white silk saree with gold, red and green embellishments, comes from the bride's mom's brother, my mama. My mother and I had gone to purchase it. Hasmukh Mama suggested, since time was short, he'd reimburse my mom later.

The wedding went smoothly. At the end of it, I was to leave with Gautam to go to his house. My belongings were packed and ready in a suitcase. A symbolic send off, the girl no longer belongs to her parents, and the home where she grew up and spent beautiful years of her childhood, is no longer "her" home.

"I was earning money and helping you. Why are you sending me away? Was I burdensome?" I asked my parents, as we walked to the car that would take me to Gautam's home.

Gautam was also sad. His uncle whispered in his ears, "You are not leaving your home, you don't have to cry. You are gaining someone today; you should be happy."

Once we reached their house, Gautam's mom and aunts performed a welcome ceremony at the door, a ceremony common in all Hindu weddings. The bride pushes over a small container full of rice, placed at the threshold, making sure the rice spills inside the house. The ceremony symbolizes the promise of the prosperity that comes with the entrance of the daughter-in-law into the family.

CHAPTER TWENTY

1982: PART 5

Gautam, my husband, whom I had known for only seventeen
days, left India three days after the wedding. He needed to get
back to the surgery residency in the Bronx, New York City. I
did not know what to feel about his departure. A fortnight ago
I didn't even know him. How could I miss someone who has
not become a habit yet?

I noticed his family and my family looking at me with
kindness and understanding. It was as if they were telling me,
"We know it is sad to watch him leave right after the wedding,
but don't worry, you'll be with him soon enough."

His parents were still in India. They were planning to stay a
few more days. I lived with them at his uncle's house. In
keeping with the tradition, his close relatives invited us for
dinner, so most evenings were filled up. After he left, I quit
working which allowed me to spend more time with his
parents before they left for San Francisco. My father-in-law,
who loved to talk, kept giving me more details about their life
in America. During one of his speeches, I learned he had not
yet found work in America. That explained why they were in
no hurry to return.

One day, a courier came to the house. He was looking for me, which was surprising because, other than our relatives and a few friends, no one knew I lived there. The courier delivered a letter offering me the position of account executive at the Shilpi Advertising Agency, where I had applied a few months ago. My heart sank.

While I was speechless and emotional, an uncle, Gautam's dad's cousin, who was visiting at the time, instructed me, "Tell them you will not accept because you are going to America."

I was sure this uncle believed I had gained a much better opportunity than the job at the Ad agency, which is why he insisted I not waste any time thinking about the offer.

It was not what he said that bothered me, though. I knew I couldn't accept the offer. It was how he said it. I wonder if Indian men ever understand what it feels like to put an abrupt end to a full life and start over after just getting married. Every girl in India, whose marriage is arranged to someone away from where she grew up, has to live through the experience of loss. To let go of your family, friends, work, hobbies, joys and attachments. Even the most mundane of things, along with starting a new life among strangers, makes one feel a deep sense of loss that takes a long time to recover from. I felt angry and sad at Uncle's cold demeanor.

Before leaving India, my father-in-law helped me understand the immigration process. It was easy to talk with him.

My mother-in-law was quiet and not easy to communicate with. I tried behaving with her like I did with my mother, but that didn't work. We went shopping before they left, but our choices were very different. We went to restaurants for dinner, but we did not like the same kind of food. It was stressful to be with her. She was not much for conversations and the time with her moved very slowly.

She hád a way that made me uncomfortable. She was not mean, rude, or condescending, and yet there was something about her that made it stressful. I observed how she related to other people in the same way. Her interactions with her mother-in-law, the aunt at whose house we were staying, and the other relatives who had stayed after the wedding, were all awkward.

The only time my mother-in-law, Saroj, seemed happy and cheerful was when her best friend Hasu visited with her daughter, Asooya. Hasu's husband Navneet and Gautam's dad were best friends since their college time. I learned from their conversations, the two couples spent many evenings together, enjoying street foods near Law Garden. They liked the same kind of spicy and oily foods. They also enjoyed playing cards. Besides Asooya, they had two boys, and the two families spent so much time together Asooya knew Gautam well and didn't hesitate showing off.

At one of their visits, Asooya asked my advice on getting admission in the school where I went for my MBA. She said the program had become very popular and was even harder than when I applied, to get an admission. I shared my experience with her.

After Gautam's parents left, his uncle suggested I go back to my parent's home to enjoy the last few days with them. Once the call for visas came from the American Consulate, I wouldn't have much time to spend with them. I was happy to go home.

But that did not last long. Whenever Gautam wanted to talk with me, he had to call at his uncle's home because my dad didn't have a phone service. So I had to return to his uncle's house.

In our phone conversations, he gave me advice to prepare me for my life in the United States. We barely knew each other, so most of his advice was not applicable to me. He asked me to take lessons to learn conversational English. He attended Sharda Mandir School, where everything was taught in Gujarati language. He didn't know I'd been speaking in English since I was six years old.

I received my visa call in June. The process involved going for an interview at the U. S. Consulate in Bombay. My Motabhai accompanied me when I went for the visa call. Before the interview, I had to fill out some forms in English. Once I finished filling them out, I noticed an elderly lady struggling with her forms. She did not know English, and no one was allowed in the room with us where we were asked to wait. I helped her with her forms.

There was a young man sitting in a corner of the room. He watched us finish our forms. When we were done, he came over to talk to me. He told me he was impressed with my willingness to help the lady.

He looked very familiar. "Have I met you before?" I asked.

He smiled. He wanted me to guess the reason for his familiarity. I couldn't.

"You have seen me on the billboards advertising men's clothing." He told me with a smile on his face. "I knew you would remember me as soon as I told you."

It surprised me he was going to America, leaving behind lucrative work. I asked him, "You have a successful career. Why are you going to America?"

His response was even more baffling. "Modeling is my hobby. I am an orthopedic surgeon." He continued, "I want to go to America and train to be an orthopedic surgeon in New York."

I told him about my husband; a doctor from India doing surgery residency in New York. I bragged about how he had landed a position in the residency program at the Bronx

Lebanon Medical Center, ten days after arrival from India. I gave him my husband's name and suggested he look for him when he came to the Bronx hospital.

Shortly thereafter, I was called in for the interview, which didn't take long.

My brother and I went back to Ahmedabad.

I left India on June 30, 1982.

CHAPTER TWENTY-ONE
NEW YORK 1982: PART 1

The flight landed at New York City's J.F. Kennedy Airport a little before midnight. I had left the only home I'd ever known, finished my first flight I had ever taken, and arrived in a new country. Now, I was about to meet my husband, a man I barely knew.

I was nervous. I was excited. I was scared. But most of all, I was tired. The long flight, the uncomfortable seating, not being able to sleep on the plane, and not having showered for over twenty-four hours added to my intense fatigue.

I just wanted to go home, wherever it was, shower and sleep.

Unsure of what to do and where to go next, I followed other passengers through immigration and the baggage claim.

"Welcome to the United States of America," the Immigration Officer said while stamping my passport. I was happily surprised at his friendly behavior and the organized and smooth fashion in which the long lines of passengers were managed. It was a stark contrast with how bureaucracy worked in India.

It took a long time to come out of the custom's department.

The plane was large, with many passengers and many international flights arriving at the same time. Some seemed happy, while others seemed frustrated. I overheard the conversation of one couple who got in trouble for bringing spices and pickles in their luggage.

"They open our bags and throw away all our Indian groceries," said one middle-aged lady wearing a saree.

"Don't worry," her husband assured her. "I'll go to the front of the line and find out if that's what's going on."

I was not worried because I didn't bring much, but having to wait in the long line made me impatient and expect the worst. When it was my turn, they asked me if I had anything in my bags that was not allowed. I kept a straight face and replied, "No, Sir." I was allowed to walk away without opening my bags.

As I made my way out of the immigration department, baggage claim and into the terminal, I was worried if I would recognize Gautam. After all, I had been with him for only two weeks. Then, I saw him waiting for me. He looked tired but happy to see me.

"I've been waiting for this day with such excitement, you have no idea," he said, as we hugged. I didn't know what to say in response because I didn't know how I felt. I wanted to feel like a new bride meeting her husband after a long time, and I was love-sick, but I didn't feel those emotions.

"Make sure you apply for your brother as soon as you get there." My father's words kept playing in my brain like an old Bollywood song.

My hug to Gautam was sincere, though. I was going to care for him and we were going to make a life for ourselves. I knew for sure. Soon, we were on our way to his home in his maroon Chevy Malibu station wagon.

"My Attending reminded me to leave for the airport," he said. "We were very busy."

The practicing physician under whom he was being trained had to remind him? Did he just forget? Was he happy to see me? I was too exhausted to figure it out.

The drive from the JFK airport to the apartment in the Bronx took two hours. I couldn't stop looking out the window. The highways, their condition, the smooth flow of traffic, the way the drivers followed the driving signals and road signs, and the number of lanes was impressive. There was no cacophony of honking vehicles, no animals around the corners, no two-wheelers weaving in and out in front of our car.

I had been transported into a totally different world.

When we reached Selwyn Avenue, I remembered the name from his address and knew home was close by. After Gautam parked his car, we walked in through the glass doors of the apartment building and took the elevator to the eighth floor

The size of the elevator surprised me. It was much bigger than the ones I had seen before. While only two people plus the lift attendant on a stool could barely fit in Indian lifts, this one could fit at least ten people and there was no attendant inside. We reached the eighth floor, and after taking less than ten steps on the carpeted hallway to the right, he stopped and unlocked the door. I entered my American home.

It was a one-bedroom apartment. Gautam gave me a quick tour making sure to let me know when he had free time, he had stocked up the refrigerator with groceries.

What jumped out at me were the stacks and stacks of magazines everywhere. Growing up in a small home, I was raised to keep things in order. Everything had a place and Mom trained us to put things away.

Our apartment faced Selwyn Ave. The bedroom and living

room had large glass windows. Looking down from them, the entrance to the hospital emergency room was in clear view.

Next, Gautam showed me the bathroom. It was big compared to our bathroom in India. He explained how to turn on the water in the shower, which was good because there were too many faucets. I would never have known what to do with them. He said the left one was for hot water, the right one for cold water, and water would come out of the shower head above by pressing the thing on the faucet.

Before I went for a shower, he told me, "I am starting plastic surgery rotation in a hospital far from here, so I will have to leave early in the morning."

I didn't know what that meant, so I didn't worry about it. I just knew it felt good to have a long hot shower. When I finished, he was fast asleep.

The next morning I woke up to an empty apartment. Gautam must have left early, just as he had said.

I looked around. "Now what?" I asked myself.

I could not call my parents to let them know I had reached safely. They did not have a phone. I did not know how to use the phone in America, anyway. "Who do I ask?" No answer.

I started unpacking. As I emptied my suitcases, I looked around for places to put my stuff.. There were things everywhere. I was not sure if it would be all right with Gautam if I rearranged the closet and other spaces.

In the kitchen, I did not know how to use the stove to cook. It seemed so big compared to the Indian stoves. I had never seen one that worked with electricity before. How can a stove turn on with a knob?

"My daughter will be a professional who will wear a pant-suit to work," Dad used to say. Against Mom's desires to teach me cooking, He had always encouraged me to focus on education and career. I knew the basics, but was not proficient in making a full meal. I was lost in my new kitchen.

I did try to cook dinners for a few evenings, but by the time Gautam came home he was too tired to care about eating. He tried to seem interested in what I had made. Most nights he would be so late, he had already eaten hot-dogs from the street vendor or food from the cafeteria where he worked. After that, I lost whatever little interest I had in making dinners.

"I bought this Zenith TV from an Indian store in Queens last week, just for you," Gautam said with pride. "You can watch it to learn about America and the way they talk. It will help you pick up the accent and slang." I started eating Chips-Ahoy cookies and milk for dinner while watching TV.

When Gautam's dad came to convince me to marry him, he claimed their large, close-knit family would be my support in a land far away from my place of comfort. "Sarojben (he used to call my mother-in-law by her name, which was not a normal practice in Indian culture) will come to visit you when you arrive. She will orient you to the way of life in America," he had promised. But she did not come. She only called me once right after I arrived. No uncles, aunts, or cousins called to talk with me.

I was lost. The thoughts of having made a big mistake started haunting me. Why did I agree to this marriage? I could have worked at the advertising agency where I had been offered a job. I had a great life, friends, parents, and a career. I had a perfect life.

I considered going back to India.

"You knew what you were getting into," Gautam would say when I expressed my feelings. "You are free to go back, if that is what you want."

I was angry with him and asked him again and again,

"Why did you come to India to get married if you knew you would not have time for a new person in your life?"

I considered going back to India as he suggested. But there were too many things to consider. "Dad wants me to bring *Motabhai* to America. Didn't he insist I should file his sponsorship papers at JFK airport before going home with my new husband?"

In Indian culture, once a daughter is married, she belongs to the husband's family. Her parent's home is no longer hers. Leaving her husband's home and going back to her parents' would bring shame and disrespect to the parents' family. Besides, I had too much pride and self-respect to accept I was a failure. Returning to India was not an option.

I went into a deep depression. Most days I did not wake up till mid-day. Then, I would look down from the glass windows and watch the hustle and bustle in the emergency room. At first my imagination about the injured and bloody bodies coming out of the ambulances frightened me.. Gradually I got used to the screeching sounds of the ambulances and police cars. It must have been a good six months before I realized it was time to pull myself together and make my own path in this new world.

CHAPTER TWENTY-TWO

1982: PART 2

Sometimes Gautam called to make sure I was ok. He advised me to stay in the apartment. "There are a lot of tall and big black men in this area. They know the young brides from India have a lot of gold. Remove the gold jewelry you are wearing, when you leave the apartment so you don't draw attention to yourself. They will rob you and rape you, so better yet, don't go anywhere."

"When will you come home?" I asked, feeling lonely.

"I will not be home till late evening. This new rotation is intense and the hospital is far." As if that was supposed to make sense to me. "But don't leave home, ok. I bought the TV last month, just for you. Watch TV so you can learn about life in America."

He came home at around nine pm. He looked exhausted. Seeing him like that, I realized my anger had to be put away. I was upset but he had been honest about his schedule with me, so there was no point in discussing anything.

"I'll leave tomorrow at five am as well, and come home around the same time as today. Then the day after tomorrow, I'll be on call so I won't come home at night."

"You mean not come home at all, or come even later? What is *a call*?" I asked, trying to understand.

"A call is when I have to take care of the patients who come to the emergency room. I could be needed at short notice so I have to stay there at night." He was tired from the fourteen-hour workday. Without another word, he was asleep.

I had so many questions for him. Did he have friends? Will my life be like this all the time? How will I find a job? If, I cannot leave this apartment, how will I learn to live in this new country? Why did your father say you were going to help me settle down and also go with me to England to see my brother? When will your mother come to orient me for my life here, as was promised by your dad?

He never seemed to have the time or energy to answer any my questions.

I had been picked up from one universe and dropped into a totally different one in a blink of an eye. Until now, no one from my circle of friends and relatives had gone to America. I had never any heard stories about life here.

I had never been away from my family. My parents and my brother, Mayank, were always there for me. I was a cherished daughter and sister. My life was full of friends and family who adored me.

I had never had a relationship with someone of the opposite gender, other than the one I had with my brother, father, uncles and male cousins.

Suddenly, I was living on the eighth floor of an apartment building in the Bronx, with a man who was practically a stranger. I had to learn about a new country, a new profession, and a new man in my life all at once. There was no one to talk to or get help from. My dad's home in India did not have a phone line. Only one of his friends had a phone line at his home. If I wanted to call my family, I had to send a letter with an instruction for them to be available at my dad's friend's home at a future date on which I would call.

I was lonely and frustrated. Not knowing or understanding how to live a normal life began to take its toll.

CHAPTER TWENTY-THREE

1982: PART 3

After a few days in the apartment in the Bronx, the basket where I was told to put the dirty clothes was full. I felt unsettled about it but didn't know what to do. I wondered if Gautam would ever the have time to show me how to wash the clothes.

I remembered his mother had mentioned something about it before she left India. "In America, machines do everything, wash dishes and clothes. They even clean the floor."

In India, we washed our laundry on an elevated block of concrete every day. I liked helping my mom. First scrubbing, then beating with a solid flat wooden bat, and then rinsing them off in a bucket. Once all the clothes were washed and collected in a bucket, they would all be hung on a clothesline to dry.

Our landlord never got the washing area cleaned properly and little mushrooms grew over the cover of the gutter, where the dirty water drained. I hated those mushrooms and tried very hard to keep my eyes from looking in that corner.

Since my arrival in America, I spent many hours of the day

looking for ways to kill time and yet the dirty clothes kept piling up. I felt useless.

"Can I wash these clothes in the apartment?" I asked my husband one day.

"You want to do a wash, huh?" He sounded amused.

"Yes, I do. I am looking for things to do. I am bored."

On his way out to work, he pointed to a huge jar of coins. "There is a laundry room in the basement of our building. Take the elevator and push the button with the letter B on it, it will take you to the basement. Turn left and you will see the laundry room. Take the basket of laundry, the detergent from the closet and coins," he said as he went out the door.

My heart was full of excitement. I was going to leave the apartment and do something of value. Something useful.

I quickly found out it was not going to be easy to take the coin jar, basket full of clothes, and detergent. But I tried. I am sure people with me in the elevator had many questions about my sanity but thankfully no one expressed them.

I managed to reach the laundry room in the basement and noticed huge white machines that looked like short cabinets. I gave myself a tour of the room. Some machines were labeled washers and some, dryers. Through a glass door on one machine I assumed to be a dryer, I saw clothes getting tossed up and down. I thought how interesting. "How can tossing clothes around and around dry them?" Then, I touched the door and it felt warm. This was definitely different from how we dried clothes in India.

I did not know how to use these machines and there was no one there to ask. I was not about to carry the jar of coins, the laundry basket and the detergent back to the apartment. I picked one machine labeled washer and started to read the instructions.

The instructions said to put three quarters, one in each of

the slots. I did not know what a quarter looked like. I looked at all the coins in the jar, took one of each size and went back to the washer. The quarter coins fit in the three slots and I confirmed the accuracy by looking at the coin to make sure it was called a 'quarter'.

"What are you doing?" I heard a sweet female voice from behind.

"I am reading instructions on this machine," I replied, turning to her.

Standing not too far from me was this slim, tall, pretty Indian lady with a big smile on her face. Her presence felt like a bright ray of sunshine.

"I am Hetal. You must be Jyotsna. Come, I will teach you. Gautambhai did not show you?" She walked towards the washer.

Bhai is a word added after a man's name in Indian culture. It is an expression of respect towards men, almost like Mister. There is also a word we use in place of Mister, *Shree,* before a male name.

Surprised, I asked her, "You know Gautam? How did you know I am his wife?"

"When he came back from India after getting married, he brought me a large bag full of wedding pictures and two blank albums. He wanted me to put the pictures in the album. I recognize you from the pictures."

"Really?" I was surprised.

"He was supposed to let us know when you got here," she replied. Something about her demeanor was reassuring to me.

We talked for a long time. Her husband was doing internal medicine residency in the same program. She was not as lonely as I was because the internal medicine residency was less intense, only three years long, and it got easier as the residents were closer to finishing. She, unlike me, had lived in

America with her family since she was fifteen. Her parents, sister, and brother lived in Chicago.

I was watching her as she took over my washing project. The washing machine took about an hour. "Depending on what kind of clothes you are washing, you have to select the cycle," she said, pointing at the big round button which was a dial that could be turned to different labels on the washer: whites, permanent press, and so on.

"Once the wash is done and the machine stops moving, we open it and take the washed clothes to the dryer." She continued her laundry lessons. "Just like the washer, you have to select the temperature and time on the dryer depending on the type of clothes."

I was impressed at how the machines did actually wash and dry clothes. Thanks to this stranger, I learned how to use these machines.

Our laundry rendezvous ended with her offer to help me with anything and everything I needed. That evening I felt much better, happier than I had felt since I came from India.

CHAPTER TWENTY-FOUR

1982: PART 4

Driving around with Gautam (whenever he had time), I was becoming familiar with the area. Unlike my mom, I had a great sense of direction. He often pointed out landmarks, like the multi-story department store Alexander's, and the famous George Washington Bridge.

"See that store, there? It's Alexander's, a big store where you can buy everything except groceries. It has a basement where they sell merchandise at a very low price. Once, I bought some shirts for four dollars each," he proudly informed me.

One day, I collected some money lying around in the apartment and took the bus to Alexander's. I was just trying to do something instead of feeling angry and restless. It was very therapeutic for me. I got off at the bus stop and crossed the wide Grand Concourse road to reach the big department store. Crossing the busy road was enough to make my heart beat fast. In India, we didn't have lanes. Roads there were as narrow as one lane of this wide multi-lane road.

The first time I entered the multi-storied store in America, I was overwhelmed at it's size. Escalators went up to the upper floors. Wow. I rode up and down a few times. Then, I went to each floor to look at all the things on display. I didn't have money to buy anything, but I looked everywhere and at everything. I even went to the basement, where they kept things they described as "clearance." The prices of the items in the basement were very low, indeed.

After a thorough self-guided tour of the store, I asked the security man at the entrance how to find a bus to go back to where Gautam worked. The apartment building was on the street behind the hospital, so I was sure if I arrived there I would be able to get home.

With great satisfaction, I reached home safely and felt proud I was able to get out of the apartment and do something all by myself.

The Milstein Building, where we lived, housed offices up to the fourth floor. Fifth floor and above, the apartments were filled with residents, students who were learning to be different kinds of doctors after finishing medical school: internal medicine, pathology, cardiology, and surgery.

A Pakistani doctor and his wife lived on the sixth floor. I learned this when I ran into her on our elevator ride up to our respective apartments.

"Hi. You live in this building?" she asked.

"Yes, on the eighth floor. And you?" I asked back.

"I live on the sixth floor. You must be new. I have not seen you before."

As soon as I confirmed her guess, she invited me to her apartment. I had nothing to do, so I went with her. The apartment was the same size as ours, but the layout was different because, it was in another section of the building. The family room was nicely furnished and decorated. Her beautiful sofa was covered with plastic sheeting. I assumed they must not have had time to remove the plastic yet. I noticed many Indian people covered their couches with plastic so they didn't get soiled with food.

We started talking about our loneliness and boredom. She did not seem as discontent as I was. She did not want to work. She had a basic education and could speak reasonably good English. She could not wait for her husband to finish his residency so she could start a normal life with him in a safe neighborhood.

I described to her how, out of frustration, I had ventured out on my own and gone to a store named Alexander's.

"You went to Alexander's?" She jumped out of the sofa. "I love shopping. You went to the store by yourself? How did you do that? You know how to take the bus? Your husband did not mind?" Her excitement was palpable.

"I did not ask my husband," I continued. "He is never home, and I didn't want to disturb him at the hospital when I decided to go. I took the bus there. It's not that scary."

"Next time, you must take me along," she said.

"I don't care about shopping," I assured her, "but I want to learn to go places by myself. If you want to shop, we can go whenever you want." I was very proud of myself. I was the one in the know.

It did not take many days before she decided she had to go with me to the store. We left around mid-morning. I made sure she knew to bring money in the form of coins and not bills, for the bus. We got on the bus and reached the store in fifteen minutes. As soon as we got off the bus, her steps quickened.

"I have nothing in particular to buy so what department do you want to go to?"

"Oh, I want to see everything."

Watching her eyes take in everything around us I realized

there was a possibility she would wander off without me. "Let us decide to meet somewhere, in case we get separated," I suggested.

We decided to meet at the bottom of the escalator right in front of the store's main entrance.

Before I knew it, she was gone. She was like a kid in a candy store. Coming to the store not too long ago, I had no need or desire to go to every department. I decided to let her take her time and enjoy. I didn't need to follow her. Besides, we decided where to meet so it would be fine to let her be by herself.

After what I considered enough time had passed, I waited by the escalator in case she was done and ready to go home. She did not show up. I waited some more. There was no sign of her. I began to panic.

I thought, "How well do I know her? Maybe she is waiting at the end of the escalator on the first floor. After all, Americans don't number the floors like we do in India and Pakistan."

I went up one floor to look for her. She was not there. I waited. She did not show up. I went down again, assuming she had understood the floor numbering correctly. She was not there. I did not want to go too far from the escalator. I was beginning to become afraid she must have left after waiting for me. The thought scared me even more. "What if she took the wrong bus?"

I knew I was in trouble. If I didn't find her, my husband would be upset and her husband would never know what happened to her. He must never have come home to an empty apartment before. I was horrified at all these thoughts.

Not knowing who to call and how to call for help, I decided to stand next to the escalator by the front door. No one could have moved me from there. As I waited, I was reprimanding myself. "You think you are too smart. Now look at what you have done. What will you tell your husband? He will certainly send you back to India. How are you going to find your friend? Doesn't your husband have enough stress? Why did you do something to add to it?" It was as if my mother were talking to me as she did when she disapproved of something my brothers and I did.

When I snapped out of my thoughts and glanced up one more time, I saw her coming down the escalator. Her hands were full with shopping bags. She seemed tense.

"Where have you been?"

"I went to every department. It was fun. But when I came down, I didn't see you," she answered.

"I thought you must be lost, so I went looking for you. I had been waiting here for a very long time."

"It's always like that for me. When I go to a store, I take my time. I enjoy being in a store. Look at all this I bought." She pointed at the bags.

"Well, I am not like that. I was bored. When I felt like you must be done, I went looking for you. I didn't think you were still shopping. I was afraid you must be lost."

"I kept looking for you."

What turned out to be an experiment in independence for me was a fun shopping trip for her. Happy I had not lost her, we walked out of the store, took the bus, and went safely home. On the bus she showed me all her shopping. She had bought a shirt for her husband, utensils for her kitchen, flat shoes for herself and a bedsheet set.

I am not sure what she told her husband, but a few days later when he ran into my husband, he requested he keep me away from his wife.

CHAPTER TWENTY-FIVE

1982: PART 5

"You are on a twenty-four hour call every third day," I said to Gautam, a few weeks after my arrival in New York. "On other days, you leave before six in the morning and return late in the evening."

"Yes. I told you this when we met before we married." He sounded tired and frustrated.

I understood his situation quite well. He was overworked and sleep deprived. His surgery residency was a pyramid program, which meant they admitted twenty-five medical students to be trained to become surgeons, but only five would finish and graduate as general surgeons. The thought of not being able to finish generated a lot of tension. There was no time to decompress.

"Do you know how bad it is for me? Last night we had a patient with multiple gunshot wounds come in from the emergency room. The surgery went on for a very long time. I was hungry, tired, and falling asleep. I had to step out of the operating room, find a packet of sugar to keep my sugar levels up until I finished the surgery."

"What happened? Did you finish?"

"Of course, I did. But it wasn't easy."

For Gautam, it was a matter of survival. The only option he had was to not allow himself to think about how exhausted he felt.

I, on the other hand, was a mere twenty-three year old, who had no one to talk to, nowhere to go. I was stuck on the eighth floor of an apartment building located across from a busy emergency room in the Bronx. The apartment was small with one bedroom, a tiny kitchen and bathroom. It had stacks of medical journals everywhere. Archives of Surgery, Journal of American Medical Association and others. I did not know if I was allowed to move them, much less organize them. I would stare at them and wonder, "When will he have time to read them?"

Even though I never saw him read those magazines, his passion for surgery was obvious to me. He breathed surgery, he dreamed of surgeries, he loved to be in operating rooms, he kept thinking of surgeries he performed and how he could do better. He even designed a new instrument, an endotracheal tube with built in suction.

He explained how it would help surgeons do better, but since I couldn't understand anything he told me, I nodded and smiled.

One time when it was a slow day, he came home early and together we went to see an attorney who specialized in patent registration. We paid one thousand dollars to the attorney to help him with the process. Apparently the expert was supposed to research if any other applications were pending for a similar surgical tool. But lack of knowledge about the systems and limited free time resulted in dropping the idea. He told me to go to the library and look in the books about patents. But that was too much for me to understand or explore.

I admired his love for what he did but felt like I failed him.

In the beginning, the nights were scary. The sirens of the ambulances conjured up ghastly images of victims. The thought of deep sadness felt by the families of the very sick patients made my heart break. I had watched a foreign film in India, *Coma*, which had put a strong fear of hospitals in me. Now, the memories of it were coming back.

When he came home, often his scrubs would be blood stained. I did not want to touch them, let alone wash them. He smelled of the disinfectant he used to clean the surgery site. I later learnt the yellow stains and pungent smells were from the chemical called Betadine.

The few hours my husband was home, he was tired and sleepy. He did not even have the energy or awareness to find out what I had made for dinner.

I understood it took time to learn about a new place. However, I had not grasped the idea of how it would be to live with a stranger. I had visualized, in my naïve way, a life where I would be going to work at a job similar to the one I had in India within a few weeks of my arrival in America. I assumed I would embark on an adventure and share it with a friend. No big deal.

"If you knew about your life here, why did you come to India to get married?" I asked Gautam. "What were you thinking?" I put him on the spot many times. It was beyond my comprehension he would not have told his parents he didn't have time for a new person in his life.

"I told you everything," he insisted. "I described my life to you in detail. You seemed confident and ready for this life."

He had dark circles under his eyes. Often, his demeanor scared me. I had mixed feelings. I felt guilty for adding to his already high stress life and at the same time I felt betrayed and stuck.

"Yes, but there is no way I would have understood it. Your dad promised you would take me to see my brother in London." I kept going. I was restless. "How can I look for a job? I don't know anything here, and you never have time to show me how things are done."

"Ok, when we go to the bank this weekend we will pick up a job application for you. Maybe you'll be able to work there and start learning more about this country." He assured me, "Everyone goes through culture shock."

He gave me hope.

We left for the bank on Saturday in the early afternoon. Gautam was always tired, so even if we planned things on the weekends, we could never leave home in the morning.

The bank was on a major thoroughfare in the Bronx, Grand Concourse. Parking was always a problem in the Bronx. Double parking was a norm. A big chunk of his paycheck paid for parking tickets.

After finishing our personal banking, we asked the teller about a job application form. Once we left the bank, Gautam showed me the bus stop from where to take the bus to get to the bank and then the stop to catch the bus back to the apartment.

I took the bus to the bank on Monday to drop off the job application. It was my first bus ride by myself. I was a little nervous but the excitement of getting a job overshadowed the fear of the bus ride. Besides, I had exact change for the fare.

At the bank, I took a written test. It was easy. It was similar to an IQ test with many questions requiring logic to answer them, along math problems. I was sure I did well.

When I returned the answer sheet the person informed me I would get a call if I did well.

I was satisfied with the fact I had started my journey towards employment, towards settling down. I waited for a few days, almost by phone. I was a little scared and confused. I did not know how to dress for an interview. Nonetheless, I was excited I was going to start working at a bank soon because I knew I had done well on the written test.

When the phone call came I was like a little kid in the park. I took the bus to the bank, and felt like an expert in public transportation.

The manager who called me in his office was polite. He was friendly and addressed me respectfully, shook my hands and smiled a lot.

I noticed that the people here, in America, were very polite and sweet in the way they talked to other people. The security guard at the building, the bus driver, the maintenance man in the apartment building-they were all kind and polite. There was a culture, a mannerism very different from India.

The manager informed me he could not offer me a job because I was overqualified. My heart sank. "I don't mind working as a teller," I told him.

"You have an MBA. Your scores in the test are one of the few very high scores we have seen." He listed my attributes as if they were bad. "If we hire you as a teller, you'll be bored."

"You can hire me as a management trainee," I said.

"For a position in management, you need to be familiar with the American economy and business environment, and you don't have that. Sorry, we cannot offer you a job."

I took the bus home, sad and disappointed. All the depressing thoughts came back. I should never have agreed to marry. I should never have agreed to marry someone in America. His family cheated me. No one from his family was here to help me. He was never around to help me. My dad did not worry about me when he arranged this life for me. He just wanted me to come to America. What am I going to do with my life now?

I came back to the apartment, watched TV for the rest of the day, and had Chips Ahoy Chocolate Chip cookies for dinner.

CHAPTER TWENTY-SIX

1982: PART 6

I was disappointed I didn't get the bank job. But, more than disappointed, I was angry. There was no one who could guide me in looking for a job.

Gautam was always gone. He couldn't help me even if he wanted to. He barely knew anything about America. He started working in the Bronx ten days after he arrived from India, not enough time to learn anything about this place.

"The economy is really bad. Interest rates are over fourteen percent," he said. "People are losing jobs in all sectors of the economy. Unfortunately, you have come from India at the wrong time." He kept repeating what he heard people say at the hospital.

Did that mean I'd have to sit on the eighth floor of an apartment building in the Bronx waiting for the economy to get better?

I wanted to belong. I wanted to work, go places, and drive to stores. I just wanted to feel normal. In trying to get the process of assimilation going, I thought I should concentrate on one hurdle at a time and driving seemed to be the most necessary skill.

I introduced the subject with apprehension. "Gautam, my friend said I should take driving lessons."

"Do you know how much the driving lessons cost? We don't have that kind of money to spare. I'll teach you."

One Saturday, when he was not on call, we drove to the streets under an elevated rail line. Once he parked, he got out of the driver's seat and told me to get in it. He sat next to me and explained how automatic cars worked. He told me about the basic rules of driving and to start driving straight.

He had a Chevy Malibu station wagon, a huge car compared to the Fiats I had seen in India and even bigger than the Vespa I used to drive. I was afraid and could not understand the space the big car needed. The fear was overwhelming.

Being with a man I didn't know well, who panicking and picking at me for every movement I made, was not helping. He was afraid I would have an accident. I didn't blame him. Needless to say, we didn't get very far.

Eventually, I took one paid driving lesson from a professional. I learned the rules of driving in America. STOP signs means you actually have to stop, unlike in India. You can pass a car only from the left side of the slow car. If the sign says: "No right on Red," you cannot turn right even if there are no cars to be seen. One has to go to the extreme left lane to make a U-turn. So many rules and yet everyone follows them. This was a radical idea for me.

Whenever Gautam had time, we went to the empty parking lots where I would drive around while he sat next to me. He seemed calmer because he noticed I knew the rules. He emphasized the looking back over the right shoulder before turning or changing lanes on the right. Making the number eight was a big deal to him, I noticed.

He'd say repeatedly, "If you can master making a figure

eight, you have mastered driving. It means you can make any turns you need to make."

I paid attention to his instructions and worked hard to accomplish the goal.

After a few such practice sessions, and memorizing the rules in the DMV book, I was ready to get my driving license. My ticket to freedom. We went to the DMV office. I took the tests and passed. I was, now, a proud owner of a Driving License in America.

Soon my euphoria from having the license waned. I was not competent or confident enough to drive on the busy streets of the Bronx during weekdays. Besides, I had nowhere in particular to go. On weekends, if and when we left home, sleep-deprived and exhausted, Gautam did not have the patience to let me drive.

On one sunny Saturday, Gautam decided we would go to Queens for Indian groceries. "A lot of Indians live there and there are many Indian stores because of that."

"Where is Queens? Why is it called Queens? Is it another city? Is it far? Am I going to drive there?"

He looked at me with annoyance and amusement. "It is a part of New York City. It is far. No, you will not be driving because we have to drive on a freeway. People drive very fast on freeways. You are not ready." He continued, "We will need money so we'll go to the bank first."

"Where is the bank? Is it the same bank where I applied for a job? Can I drive there? I know where that is."

Again, he spoke with exasperation. "We're going to another branch of the same bank. But banks are busy on Saturdays. People double-park. You will have trouble driving. You don't have enough experience."

Yup, and this is how I am going to get experience.

As we approached the bank, I noticed he was right. The streets seemed narrow. There were cars everywhere. Cars were double -parked on every street. As we went around the bank a few times, looking for parking, he grumbled there was no spot to be found. I had learned by then parking was his pet peeve. I chose to keep strategic silence.

Determined to get cash from the bank, he stopped the car in front of the bank. "Stay in the car. I'll be right back."

"No." I panicked. "The police will come and bother me. What will I tell them?"

"As long as the car is on, it is not considered parked. That's why I want you to stay here. It won't take me long."

I didn't know the American slang back then, but I must have said something to the effect. "You've got to be kidding me. Why are the other people who have double-parked not in their cars?"

As I kept arguing, he sprinted from the car towards the bank. I sat on the passenger side of his huge station wagon, with the key in the ignition. It was horrifying. The people driving in the same direction made angry gestures because our car was in their way. I felt as if every person driving by or walking by was asking me, "Are you crazy?"

While terrified, I was also on a vigil, watching the streets with keen eyes. I saw a police car pass by on the opposite side of the street. "That's it. He's not back. I can't leave the car to tell him to come back before the police made a U-turn and came back to our car. We were in trouble."

My primal instincts took over. "When in trouble, run," my mind told me. Before I realized it, I had gotten out of the passenger side and into the driver's seat and started driving.

Honking cars driving next to me gave me no option but to turn right. Having made a few circles around the bank before going into it, Gautam had unknowingly helped me familiarize myself with the area. I kept turning right at every corner.

While circling the block I was so preoccupied with the fear of the police, I kept looking in the rear view mirror to make sure they were not following me. A small part of my brain was also thinking, "When Gautam comes out of the bank, he will not see the car. He will be worried about me. No problem, by then I will be back in front and I'll tell him to get in on the passenger side and we will drive away."

Thus, engrossed in my various thoughts, I didn't notice as I passed by the double or triple parked cars, I was scraping some of them.

After what felt like an eternity of driving, I noticed Gautam in front of the bank. His face was white with panic.

I proudly waved at him from the window of the passenger seat, while mouthing the words, "Get in, quickly."

He ran over to the car and in no uncertain terms opened the driver's side door and sternly ordered, "Get out."

"I can drive. Look how I saved us from the police," I said like an excited teenager.

"Get out and let me drive."

I stepped out of the car and went around to my assigned position. Gautam took the driver's seat and we drove on.

"I told you to stay in the car and wait." He was not angry, just confused and worried. "Why did you start driving?"

"I saw a police car. I was afraid we'd get in trouble for keeping the car in the road like that," I explained. "Before the police reached our car, I drove away. It was easy."

"As long as you were in the passenger seat, he would not have bothered you." Gautam tried to stay calm.

"But wouldn't he wait for you to come out and then give us a ticket?" I questioned his assertions. I was very certain of my logic and reasoning for driving away.

Instead of continuing to argue further, he asked, "How did you do? Were you afraid?"

"I was terrified, but I had to save us from getting another ticket. We still have so many left to pay off."

CHAPTER TWENTY-SEVEN

1982: PART 7

Sitting on the couch, staring at the television, quite often, I wondered about my future. Days were long. Time passed very slowly. There was a library around the corner from the apartment building, but Gautam had frightened me about the groups of scary, tall black men standing around there. "Don't go to the library by yourself."

"When we met for the first time, you said you would like to get more education," Gautam reminded me. "Why don't you go and check out some colleges?"

"Really? I can do that?"

"At least find out more about the courses, fees, the process for getting your Indian education evaluated and other details."

I was hopeful. The potential of finding something to advance my career or education was what I needed to feel positive and happy. The idea that after marriage, my main purpose in life would be to take care of the home and be happy in the thoughts of getting to see him for a little time, was something I had never understood. The way I saw it, I was the same person, wanting to live similar to how I lived in India. The only difference was instead of my parent's and brother's family, I was living with a friend and in another location.

I believe, for someone to have joy, one needs hope more than anything else. Hope signifies the potential for self-improvement, something happening, or coming in your life makes you want to get up in the morning.

Over the next few days, I visited Fordham University and Pace University. I went to the admission office of both colleges. The conversations went something like this:

"What do you want to study?"

"I don't know. I have an MBA in Marketing, but no one gave me a job. What should I study?"

"Have you had your transcripts evaluated?"

"What does that mean?"

"You have to send your degrees and certificates with the description of course work to an agency that evaluates education acquired in foreign countries. They will issue a certificate that will tell us how it compares to the education here. Based on that we would be able to advise you."

"How long does that take? Can you give me the name of the agency? Will they charge for this service?"

"Sure. But in the meantime, you can enroll for general ed courses."

"What is general ed?"

"General Ed is a list of courses every student takes in the beginning."

"But I am not beginning. I already have a Master's degree."

"However, you did not take General Ed courses. There is a list of courses, like US History and English 101, which you'll have to take anyway. Let's enroll you in those courses."

I was confused. I couldn't understand. Why should I spend money on courses I didn't need? We didn't have money to spare on unnecessary courses.

"What did you find out?" Gautam asked.

"I don't think I should go to college. It will be expensive. I don't know what I want to study. I can get the transcripts evaluated but that will take time. I have to ask my dad to collect the course descriptions and send them to me."

"Hmm. I don't know what to say. I'm not much help," Gautam said.

Then, he came up with an idea. "Why don't you volunteer at the hospital?"

Again, there was hope.

The very next day, I went to the office of the Department of Surgery on the fourth floor. I offered to volunteer and informed them I had good education and was willing to do any clerical work they needed help with.

Dr. Gerst, the director of the residency program for surgery, was familiar with my last name. He was the one who had given my husband admission to the surgery program.

"Let her sort and file all operation reports in the Medical Records Department," he smirked. "We'll find out how good she is."

Sorting operation reports by the doctor's name and filing them was an extremely boring job. It was challenging only due to its mass. It had not been done for a long time. The only sustaining thought that kept me going was as soon as I brought the filing up to date I could be assigned more interesting work.

Filing those reports was educational. Sometimes, I would read them, especially the ones performed by Gautam. I became familiar with medical terms and even the names of people.

New York hospitals were filled with foreign medical graduates undergoing residency training. There were doctors from the Philippines, India, Pakistan, Cuba, Columbia, Mexico, Argentina, China, Taiwan and other countries. I learned when President Lyndon Johnson created the Medicare program, the need for physicians went up creating a shortage. The U. S. Government, therefore, had to relax the immigration rules to allow foreign medical graduates to enter the country.

Working in the hospital allowed me to meet more people. I began to feel more comfortable talking with Americans. Sometimes I did not understand what they were saying, and sometimes they did not understand what I was saying, but that did not bother me.

One time, I was introduced to this nice middle-aged black lady.

"Hello Dear, I am Ms. Metz," she said sweetly.

"Ms.?" I asked.

"Ms. Metz, like the New York Mets," she replied, assuming I would know about the New York Mets. I pretended to know.

The more black women I met, the more I liked them. I loved their accent, how they talked and laughed. It sounded like music.

After I finished filing the big pile of operation reports, they moved me to the Administration Office. There, I had an opportunity to interact with and observe other women working in the office. I went through a culture shock during that time.

Some of the girls were wearing short skirts. I wondered why they felt the need to do that. In India, I dressed modestly and did not use make-up to look prettier. I did not feel the need to look feminine or sexy to survive in a man's world, and India, in the 1980s, was definitely a man's world.

I had imagined America to be a country where women were more equal to men. Where women had full freedom to achieve anything they wanted without using their appearances. Why should a secretary have to wear short skirts and tall uncomfortable shoes and spend the precious morning time putting on make-up to look presentable?

"Why are you volunteering? Don't you want to get paid?" a young, skinny lady wearing a short skirt and high-heeled shoes asked.

"I couldn't get a job."

"But, you have to have your own money. What happens if your husband does not give you any money?" She was concerned about me.

"I don't know what you mean. His money is my money."

"Oh no, you don't know if he has a girlfriend. Your marriage was arranged, right? What if he has a girlfriend and uses his money for her? You should have your own income and bank account." She did not let up.

"But he has no time for me. How can he have a girlfriend?"

"You never know about these young doctors," she continued.

The evening after this conversation, alone at home, I was not sure what to think. Nothing she had said made sense. And yet, she seemed right. I really didn't know Gautam. He may have a girlfriend. How would I have known? How would I even find out? Oh, my God, my parents did not worry about me at all when they arranged my marriage and sent me so far away from them.

It was not just that my parents didn't care, but now Dad wanted me to focus on bringing my brother to the USA. In the first letter I received a month after I arrived, he talked more about my responsibilities towards my brother and parents than about what I was going through. I was sure Dad was confident in my abilities to succeed in my new life, but he did not know much about my life here, in the US. These thoughts were depressing.

Finding a job took on a new level of urgency. "I'll have to

continue the volunteer work so they will be tempted to offer me a job," I told myself while trying to fall asleep.

Dr. Gerst liked me. He used to joke with Gautam, "You are good, but she's better." I knew he didn't mean that, but I felt good anyway. He promoted me to the work of scheduling interviews for the medical students who applied for surgery residency. It was interesting work. I was gaining insight into the world of medical education and training. It finally made sense why Gautam was proud of being in his residency program. The process of screening students, interviewing them and making a decision to admit them took one full year, and yet he was admitted without ever having applied and within ten days of arriving in New York.

I was not getting paid, but I was busy learning new things about life in the USA.

CHAPTER TWENTY-EIGHT

1982: PART 8

Working on the fourth floor was perfect. All I had to do was take the elevator down from the eighth floor. Like everyone else, I also took a lunch break at noon. At that time, I took the elevator down to the ground floor to check for mail.

Just like the road system, the mail delivery in the USA impressed me. It was very different from the Indian Postal Service. In the USA, the mailman used a car, while in India they used bicycles. The mailman in the USA wore a blue uniform, the one in India wore a khaki uniform and it included a Nehru style cap. I wondered if the cap was included to protect the mailman's head from intense summer heat, as he was exposed to the elements during his bicycle rides.

Facing the automatic glass doors to the building was a desk where the security guard sat to ensure the safety of the building residents and hospital employees who worked in the offices in the building. On the left was a hallway with two elevators. Just before the elevators, there was a small alcove where mailboxes were inside the wall. All the boxes had a keyhole. This was very different and interesting. We were given a key to the box assigned to our apartment.

I checked the mailbox every day at lunchtime, hoping to see a letter from home. Dad loved writing letters, so I often received letters from him. Mom usually wrote a sentence or two at the end.

When I received the first letter from Dad, I was excited and happy to see what he had written. I ran up to the apartment and opened it as fast as I could and started reading. It felt like he was talking to me. He was advising me not to get discouraged and sad from loneliness. "Solitude strengthens the soul," he wrote.

The rest of the letter was a reminder to me about my responsibilities as a daughter and a sister. "Now that you are settled, isn't it time for you to send a nice camera for your brother. You know how badly he has been wanting a nice camera from abroad." My heart sank.

Without the facility of a phone connection it was hard to communicate often. This made it impossible for my family to understand the daily challenges of a new place and a new life. I was not able to convey my situation and circumstances. We did not have money to spare for a "nice" camera. It saddened me to think I had to worry about my family's expectations. I was already stressed from the knowledge I had to figure out how to sponsor my brother and his family to come to the USA.

That evening, when Gautam read the letter he was very upset with my family. "I know you or they don't care about me. You married me to bring your family to America. See, now we have proof."

My family's impatience, Gautam's suspicious nature, and my lack of tact and diplomacy in keeping both sides happy made it difficult to build a relationship with my new husband.

On one Saturday afternoon, as we came out of the elevator, we ran into the orthopedic doctor I had met in the Mumbai Consulate, where I had gone for the Visa interview. I was delighted to see him and so was he, to see me. It was totally unexpected. I introduced him to Gautam, "This is my husband, who is a surgery resident in this hospital."

"Gautam, this is the doctor I told you about. He was a successful model for men's clothing in India but he wants to be an orthopedic surgeon. I had told him you can give him advice on how he can get into the residency program at your hospital." The pride about his accomplishments and the hope we could help someone was evident in my excitement.

"I don't know anything. Stay away from my wife." Gautam snapped at him as he walked away.

I was embarrassed, to say the least. I could not look at that doctor. I followed him out of the building. I felt very humiliated and confused. Why was my husband angry? Did he not trust me?

The thoughts of regret over my agreement for marriage came back.

We never talked about this incident again and he never apologized for his behavior. I didn't know how to start a conversation about it.

Then, there was Suraj. He was my dad's student and had left India long ago. Many of my dad's students left India and went abroad to different countries. Suraj was in New Jersey. On his recent visit to India, he visited Dad and found out I was in New York.

Like any dad would, my dad told him about me and was happy to send a friend my way.

Suraj called. I had a nice conversation with him and felt happy. He invited me to visit him with Gautam. When I informed my husband about it, he was not happy. "Your dad is having his students check up on me. Is Suraj going to protect you if I do something wrong?"

Everything escalated to an outburst of anger from him and I kept reacting to it. When he needed to relate to other doctors, we socialized, but I couldn't relate to the women in the group. Most of them were citizens of the USA, and the male doctors had agreed to the marriage so they would get to come to America. The women were happy to have a doctor for a husband and the men were happy to be in the USA.

I did not enjoy those gatherings. Gautam did not understand. He analyzed everything I did. "You hate doctors because your older brother could not become a doctor. You are jealous."

His habit of analyzing and putting a spin on my feelings hurt me deeply. Young and passionate, I reacted to his outrageous accusations angrily. We used to have many loud arguments.

I was very troubled. I did not understand if I should trust my instinct and believe I had made a mistake in marrying Gautam or if I was being intolerant and judgmental because I was lonely and missed my life in India. Having a lot of time by myself offered me a chance to do a lot of thinking.

I knew I had anger problems. Dad used to tell me all the time I was very sensitive. But unfair things bothered me and made me angry. In fact, my mother made my married life difficult by telling Gautam, "My daughter goes above and beyond for people she loves. But she has anger problems. Please be patient with her, you'll see she's going to be a good partner for you."

"I know you. Your mother told me you are an angry person. I don't have time for that."

"Well, I don't believe in being superficially sweet and ignoring the needs of people I love. My mother taught me actions speak louder than words."

Did all newlyweds go through such periods of tension and adjustment? Until some magic happened, the newlyweds were enemies. What should I be waiting for? What should I be doing?

CHAPTER TWENTY-NINE

1982: PART 9

My hunger for an actual job that paid me was something I could not shake off. The women I worked with at the hospital mentioned something called temp agencies. After many questions, I understood the temp agency was a place where I should send my resume. When an employer needed an employee in a hurry, or for a short period of time, the agency would match the resume with the employer's needs and call the person for an interview.

It interested me. After not getting the job with the bank, I had removed my higher credentials from my resume. I had to present myself as less qualified and apply for an entry-level job.

"How do I find temp agencies?" I asked Cheri, the lady I volunteered for, at the hospital.

"Oh, that's easy. Just look in the yellow pages," Cheri said in a matter-of-fact manner. I didn't blame her for assuming I would know what she meant.

Not ashamed to seem ignorant, I asked, "What are yellow pages?"

She pulled out a big, thick book full of lists of names and phone numbers. The first part of the book had white pages, and was a directory of all the phone numbers in the area, and the last third was yellow. "There is an alphabetical list of businesses in this book. You will find the list of all temp agencies."

I thought to myself, "One more thing about America to be amazed about."

When Gautam came home that evening, I excitedly told him about the yellow pages and the temp agencies. "Do we have yellow pages? I need to find a temp agency and take my resume to them."

"I believe I showed the phone book to you a while back, but perhaps it was too early at the time," he replied. "Anyway, here it is. Some of the agencies may be too far away and in unsafe areas, so be careful. I would take you but they all close at 5 pm, long before my day ends."

Well, wasn't that the root of all my problems!

The next day, I opened the yellow pages to find the list of temp agencies. I called a few, but couldn't explain my circumstances and expectations over the phone. I would have to go in person to drop off my resume. Opening the subway map, I started locating the addresses of the agencies.

I decided to take my resume to the agencies that were located on the subway routes most familiar and centrally located in Manhattan.

This was a unique experience for me.

I never did get a call from any agency but the process kept me from feeling helpless and allowed me to become familiar with the city.

After a few weeks without results, the depression from isolation and the sense of failure crept in again. Sometimes, it was so bad that even if Gautam planned going out on the weekend, I didn't enjoy it. We didn't understand each other. We talked, but nothing was said or heard.

CHAPTER THIRTY

I enjoyed volunteering and staying busy. Ever so curious, I remained happy as long as I was learning something new. It helped me from thoughts of remorse and regret.

At lunch, I went down to check on the mail. I even started paying bills. After opening the envelope, I'd look at the due date, write a check for the amount on the bill, use the envelope that came with it, put a stamp on the top right corner of the envelope, seal and drop the envelope in the box downstairs, labeled "Outgoing Mail." The American postal/mail system impressed me just as much as the roads and highway systems.

When Gautam was on call, he didn't come home in the evenings so I had no one to be with. Residents in other medical specialties often came home even during their on-call evenings. Surgical residents had to be available to operate at short notice on patients coming through the emergency room and therefore they could not leave the hospital.

I began doing laundry in the evenings when Gautam was on call. After all, like any other American, I was a working woman and had no time to wash laundry during the day.

Besides, there was always security at the entrance and I was not afraid to go to the basement at a late hour.

One evening, when I reached the laundry room, it was empty. As I filled the washer with clothes, a black man entered. He didn't have a laundry basket or anything related to laundry in his hands. He walked up to me and started chatting.

Having concluded that he was not there to do laundry made me nervous. My heart was racing like a deer wanting to escape a predator. Despite the fact he was polite and friendly, I felt uncomfortable talking with him.

As always, I brought a book with me to read while doing the wash. There was no one in the apartment so why not wait in the laundry room and keep up with the washers and dryers? But that day my instincts advised me to leave. While still being friendly so as not to make him aware of my suspicion, I kept walking out of the room towards the elevators. He kept going with me.

At that time of the day, it was just us taking the elevator to go up. Not wanting to ride with him all the way to the eighth floor ,I pressed "L" for the lobby and quickly got off the elevator. I was afraid he might catch on I suspected him. At the same time, I was terrified of his intentions.

I remembered my mother's advice from childhood. "If you ever get cornered by a bad man, find a way to kick him between his legs." I kept hoping I would not have to go that far.

I pretended I was leaving the building, hoping he would stop following me. As I left the building, I ran across a large group of people in white lab coats walking in. I turned around and followed them to the lobby area. They stopped in front of the elevators. Hoping I would not be alone in the elevator with him, I joined them. From the corner of my eye, I noticed he also got on the elevator. In a state of panic, I had forgotten the hospital offices only went to the fourth floor. They all pushed button number four and I pushed button number eight. My follower did not push any buttons. Once the elevator closed, I had very few seconds to consider my next move.

I was terrified and made no attempt to hide it. I kept looking at him. I thought about telling the people in the elevator about my suspicions. Somehow, I did not think they would believe me because he really had not done anything substantial to me. He had not even touched me. What would I tell them?

However, I was sure the intimidating man knew Gautam was not home. What should I do? Do I confront him? What if he had no ugly motive like the one I was assuming, and by confronting him I'd actually give him the wrong idea? I didn't know what to do.

Once the crowd of white coats got off the elevator on the fourth floor, it was just him and me. He kept looking at me. He did not act friendly and polite anymore. It seemed he was feeling secure about his plan. He had me cornered.

As we passed the fifth floor, I lunged towards the elevator panel and quickly hit the button labeled "7." The action was swift and unpredictable for him. Before he realized what I had done, the elevator stopped. The door opened to the seventh floor. I ran out, made a left, and ran as fast as I could to the end of the building.

I knew a Gujarati pediatrician and his wife lived in that apartment which was in the long wing of the C-shaped building. I banged on their door, loud enough the people across and next them also heard it. I wanted to make sure someone was available to help before the stranger reached me.

I relayed my complete story to them. The good doctor went with me to the laundry room, helped me gather my things and dropped me off at my apartment. He made sure the door was properly locked, tested it by trying to open it and instructed me to call him if the black stranger showed up at my door during the night.

This was one of the most horrifying experiences I had since I arrived in America. I stayed up all night wondering if I was being judgmental and prejudiced because of his color. He had not harmed me in any way. Was I assuming too much? I was also afraid Gautam would be upset when he found out I went to the basement so late at night. I was upset with myself I was adding stress to his already difficult life.

When he came home, I told him about my terrifying experience. He went straight to the security desk in the lobby to confront them.

"How can this happen? My wife was home alone. What are you doing here? How can a criminal pass by and reach the laundry room? Can you imagine what he would have done to her if she had not outsmarted him?"

"Doc, calm down." The security officer was in control. "We understand how you feel."

"No, you don't understand how I feel." Gautam would not let the officer continue to talk. There was nothing the officer could have said that would have satisfied him.

I understood his anger. But I was also aware if he did not stop attacking the officer, there was not going to be a resolution to the problem. I tried to calm him. At first, he ignored me but eventually he listened.

"Sir, since we check the ID badge of every person that enters the building, it is likely the stranger was an employee of the hospital." He turned to me and asked, "Can you describe this person who followed you?"

I did my best to describe the man: average height, a little shorter than me, African American, dark skin, not skinny but not fat either, very pleasant looking face and mild demeanor. "I think the name on his badge was Clyde."

As soon as I described the stranger, there was an expression of relief on both officers' faces. "We know who you're talking about."

They said the wrong words.

"You mean you know this man?" Gautam thundered with his question. "If you know a hospital employee is known to be a criminal, why is he still working here?"

"Doc, let us first have your wife identify him. We'll bring him in."

Then the officers turned to me and started asking me the specifics of the encounter. "Did he touch you? Did he say anything to you that would imply he meant to harm you? Did he threaten you in any way?"

I had no chance to respond as Gautam interjected more questions. "What do you mean? Does he have to rape her before you take action?"

"Legally, there would be no grounds for us to arrest him if she answers in the negative to any of these questions. However, we will question him once your wife identifies him," the officer explained.

"Well, then, this is useless," Gautam said, expressing his disappointment. He turned to me and continued, "They are not going to take any action against the criminal, and therefore we have no sense of security in this building anymore." He walked away in a rage, leaving me alone.

I followed him, almost running, as he got on the elevator.

"We'll have to move away from here. Once they question that guy, he will know you complained. That means you are at a higher risk. He will get away with intimidating you on a regular basis."

"I think, now I have complained, he will be afraid to bother me." I tried to reason with my husband. "I'll be ok. Look, he failed already. I've learned my lesson. I'll be cautious and vigilant. Moving will be very stressful for you. You will have to drive to work. Any place in the Bronx will be the same problem, at least here we have security."

"We'll move to New Jersey. It'll be safer there."

"But that means you'll have to cross the George Washington Bridge and you know the traffic is always backed up on it. It's ok. You're overreacting. I'll be fine. I promise I will follow very strict safety rules. You don't get enough sleep, as it is. It will be worse for you if we move. Also, I'll be isolated. There is no subway in NJ. I won't be able to volunteer anymore. What will I do all day?"

"We can sort those details out, once we are in a safe area." He was adamant.

We spent the next few weeks exploring the townships in New Jersey close to the George Washington (GW) Bridge. On weekends, any spare time he had after recovering from his sleep debt, was filled with thoughts of moving out of the Bronx. We explored apartments while arguing about the wisdom of moving out of the subsidized apartment conveniently located across the street from where he worked.

Thoughts of moving away from the one place I'd worked hard to familiarize myself with, brought back the separation anxiety I'd felt when I first arrived. I was familiar with transportation and busy volunteering. There were people I knew. The thought of losing all I had once again brought back sad memories.

During the weeks we looked for apartments, the Security Department of the Hospital found the man I had described and had me go in to make identification. Once I acknowledged it was the same person they had suspected, they warned him one more complaint of similar behavior would be the last before being arrested.

It turned out many single nurses living in the building had made similar complaints about him. He had a pattern of intimidating women but never crossed over to a behavior that would warrant an arrest.

We ended up moving to Little Ferry, a small town in New Jersey. There, I had even more time alone. Gautam left for work very early in the morning. Although the distance was short, because of the traffic on the bridge, it took him about ninety minutes to reach the hospital. I was even more lonely. My logical mind accepted and appreciated the fact my husband cared about my safety and was willing to suffer the hardship of having to commute to work. But that didn't mean I was happy.

CHAPTER THIRTY-ONE
NEW JERSEY 1983: PART 1

We moved to 279 Liberty Street, Little Ferry, New Jersey. I must admit it was a nice, quiet town. The L-shaped apartment building sat on the corner of Liberty and Main Street. Being only a block away from Route 41, made the streets very busy. I didn't mind at all, because it gave me a sign of life outside of the apartment.

We got an apartment on the first floor. The staircase opened into a large family room, and a door on the right opened into the kitchen, which was also bigger than the kitchen in our apartment in the Bronx. The living room had a large window overlooking the parking lot. Sitting on the couch by the window, I could see the traffic on the busy streets.

On the right, next to the kitchen, was a bathroom and on the left, the bedroom. The walls were the usual off-white color and the windows had ivory-colored blinds. The kitchen appliances (stove, refrigerator and microwave) were white and since the kitchen was long and rectangular in shape, there was a nice, long counter with a white Formica top starting from the refrigerator to the stove which was at the end by the window. It was a little bigger and more comfortable for us.

I continued to look for work. I found a Temp Agency run by an Indian so I called. Finally, someone who understood what I was saying without having to repeat myself. He advised me to go to his agency with my resume so he could explain how things worked in America.

When Gautam came home, I told him about my latest discovery. He was happy for me but when he looked at the address he suggested I wait. "It is too far by subway and also not a very safe area, let me take you there."

I couldn't imagine what he must have had to do, how many favors to ask, but Gautam did manage to come home early. "Be ready to come down and get in the car," he instructed. "Then we can reach there before five pm."

The drive to the agency was like driving in a race. Too much rush-hour traffic everywhere. He was trying his best but was not sure if we would reach on time. "I hate big cities. Look at this traffic. I hope he waits for us."

We barely reached the place. When we entered the office, a small room with a desk, the owner of the agency was preparing to leave. It didn't seem like he had any employees. He was kind and friendly and stated he was in touch with many Indian business owners and would try to find me a job.

I was very happy that evening. Gautam helped me and there was hope.

The Indian Employment Agency did not take long to call me. "I asked around among Indian business owners. Mr. Dalal, who owns an import business, said he would like to meet you." He continued, "He imports fabrics from India. His office is in Manhattan. Would you be interested? He will not pay a lot but you will get a start."

I was too excited to care about the pay. I wanted to say "yes" but I didn't know if I should. "I will ask my husband and call you."

I couldn't wait to tell Gautam about the good news. I was a little worried because he might refuse to allow me to work. Always tired, he was easy to get impatient and annoyed.

I tried, anyway. "Gautam, the Indian Agency called. There is a man who owns a fabric import business in Manhattan. He wants to meet me."

"Where in Manhattan? Did he give you an address?"

"I didn't ask. He said something about forty-second street."

"I don't know about this. Forty-second street is shady. Many dangerous sections on it." He was concerned. "I don't trust this guy."

"I can call him and get full address." I thought the Broadway Theater was on 42nd street. Hmmm...

The next day I called the agency. I also told them about the concerns my husband had expressed.

"Oh no, his office is in a nicer area. Tell your husband it is near Grand Central Station. It'll be fine. I know this gentleman. He owns the Gaylord Indian Restaurant, as well. Nice family."

Upon learning the new details, Gautam approved of my meeting with Mr. Dalal.

My excitement knew no limits. I figured out the way to get to A & S Fabrics. First I'd take the bus from NJ, then the subway, and then walk. That was the easy part.

I was more worried about what to wear to the interview. Observing the women where I had volunteered at the hospital, I realized I didn't have such clothing. I wasn't going to wear the short skirts and high heeled shoes. I did have some slacks and tops. Still, no shoes would look proper at work. "I am just going to meet him," I told myself. "I don't have a job yet. It's ok."

The office building was a tall narrow building, very old and dark. The office was on the second floor. The elevator was small, like the ones in India. I was greeted by an elderly lady, Suham.

"I have come to see Mr. Dalal."

"Wait here." The room was square with two desks, one right by the door and another a few feet from there, next to another door that was closed. Behind the desks were two large windows looking out into the city. Across from the them was a wall with chairs lined along it. A three-foot space parallel to the wall and in front of the desks made a passage to enter the other offices inside. I sat on one of the chairs. This was my first introduction to a business office.

Suham got up from that far desk and went behind the closed door

A few minutes later, a man my dad's age with a cigar in his mouth, wearing a three-piece suit, greeted me with a cheerful demeanor. "Hello, Jyotsana. Come follow me."

I followed him behind the door as he entered his lavish office. It had a heavy desk, chairs and bookcases. All of the furniture was dark. The chairs were of solid wood and black leather with brass nail heads lined in an ornate and immaculate manner. The desk was covered with a black leather piece, leaving the wood all around it making a border.

"Sit down, my dear." He was very friendly. "First of all, I am going to call you Jyoti. Jyotsana is too long and Americans will not be able to say it." He didn't ask, he decided.

I didn't know what to say, so I said nothing.

"You want to work? How long ago did you come from India? You are very young."

It was easy to talk with him. I did not feel nervous at all. We talked for a while about my situation, my husband's busy schedule, my attempt at getting work in the bank, my background in India, my education.

"I can give you a job. You can answer phones and help

Suham in whatever she needs." He continued, "I will pay you five dollars per hour."

It was the happiest day for me. I had not expected a job.

"In six months, if I like your work, I will raise your pay to six dollars," he continued.

I was so excited I didn't remember much about my ride home.

CHAPTER THIRTY-TWO

1983: PART 2

I was very excited about going to work in Manhattan.

On the first day, I left early. From the bus station in New York, I took the train to the subway stop closest to where I worked. From there, I had a short walk to the office.

I felt the thrill of a new "actual" job walking from the train station. The perfectly intersecting streets intrigued me. They were like the squares in a cake pan. Many corners had small shops selling newspapers and magazines while others had a hotdog stand.

Trying to get to their jobs on time, people walked at a fast pace. You could tell a train had arrived underground at the subway station from the number of people rushing up the stairs. Some with bagels held in napkins and a briefcase or a purse in the other. Women often wore sneakers with their smart looking skirt suits. At first it seemed strange but then I figured out they wanted to be comfortable for their long walk to work but changed into high heels once they reached their office. I started doing that, too. I felt smart.

In winter, the steam rising from underground through the manhole covers looked impressive, the image implying a well-designed infrastructure. Tall, smart men in long coats over handsome suits and ties, looked like characters I'd seen in foreign movies my dad used to take us to. There were many black people, as well. Despite my experience in the Bronx, I was not afraid of them.

I loved all of it.

At work, I was learning to be a secretary the American way. In addition to Mr. Dalal and Suham, three salesmen worked there; two of them, Ashok and Dipak, were of Indian background. Harry was an American. They had their regular customers they managed. Most of them were famous designers I had heard or read about.

Every morning Dipak went straight to the coffee machine. Ashok went to his office first, left the newspaper he purchased from one of the corner stands, and then came to the coffee machine. I watched them making coffee and wondered why anyone would like it. The black coffee tasted bitter to me even after adding the dry milk and sugar. In India we made it by adding instant coffee and sugar to boiling milk. Now, that was coffee worth drinking.

Harry was tall and white. He had kind eyes. He was also much older than the two Indian guys. I felt comfortable with him because of his eyes and mannerisms. He was always smiling, and unlike Suham, he didn't seem like he didn't want me there.

At first, I did not know how to answer the phones, yet that was my job. Suham watched me from the corner of her eyes every time the phone rang.

I would greet the caller, "A and S Fiber, good morning."

"Jyoti, tell them your name," Suham would remind me in a stern voice.

After a few reminders, I mastered the art of answering phones. Little did I know I had many more things to learn.

One day the phone rang. The caller was Harry's client. Before I put the caller on hold, Suham told me Harry had called and informed her he was sick.

"Sir, Harry called this morning. He said he is very sick and will not be coming to work. I don't think you will be able to talk…….."

"Jyoti, you don't have to go on and on, only tell them Harry is out sick," Suham instructed me in an angry tone.

I went back on the phone and repeated what she told me. The caller quickly thanked me and hung up. I learnt that day there were very specific phrases Americans used to convey a message and I needed to learn them. Although she never smiled at me, I knew Suham would teach me many such things.

A few months into the job, just when I was beginning to feel like my life in America was starting, just when I felt like I belonged, and I was going to be alright, we found out I was pregnant.

CHAPTER THIRTY-THREE

1983-84

I was devastated. I was supposed to feel happy about the prospect of becoming a mother but I was not. I was not ready. I was angry at Gautam.

"I don't know what I am doing here. I barely know how to live my life in America. You are never there for me. I finally have a proper job after having searched for so long. Now, I have to stop everything and become a mother." I lashed out.

"I know you feel overwhelmed," he assured me. "But you'll be alright."

"Why should I believe anything you say? I don't trust you." I was beside myself. "You and your dad lied to convince me to marry you. Once I got here none of you cared. You all brought me here as an educated maid. Now, I'm supposed to give your family a grandchild." I was crying, "You all lied to my parents so you could use me. Now I'm trapped."

"That is not fair. You are being mean to me. I didn't force you to marry me. Your family wanted you to come to America. That's why you are here."

"But they trusted you to take care of me. And you are not doing that."

We argued for hours. Part of my brain was telling me to shut-up and let him rest because he had to go to work early in the morning. The other part was filled with hate.

I hated that he didn't wait to marry until his residency was done.

I hated my friend Hetal who advised me to not take birth-control because she said she couldn't have children after taking it for a few years.

I hated my parents for sending me away from them.

I hated that they didn't care I didn't want to go to America.

I hated I was pregnant.

Soon, I reasoned myself into accepting reality. I told myself I was not meant to have a career or a professional life in America. My education and my glorious career were but a dream that evaporated at the end of a restless night of sleep.

I informed Mr. Dalal once I had the baby I'd quit working. He didn't seem surprised. He probably had seen many young, promising women from India go down the same path.

I learned how people celebrated Christmas at work. Suham ordered some cookies and made some at home. All the cookies had shapes, colors, or decorations on them that depicted the Christmas spirit. There was wine, hot apple cider, and of course, coffee, to have with the cookies. I didn't know I was supposed to bring gifts, but everyone else brought Christmas gifts for each other. Dipak and Ashok gave me perfumes, my first in America. It reminded me of Diwali celebrations not too long ago, my last one before I left. I missed home.

Six months passed. I believed I was doing a great job. I remembered Mr. Dalal's promise to give me one dollar more if he liked my performance.

"Mr. Dalal, can I speak with you for a minute?" I asked him when it was not very busy in the office.

"Sure, Jyoti," he responded with the cigar in his mouth. He

had a very easygoing and non-threatening demeanor. "Come on in."

"Yes, what can I do for you?" He was curious.

"You said if you liked my work, in six months, you would pay me six dollars an hour," I was not afraid to remind him. "Do you think I am doing a good job?"

"Ah, you remember," he exclaimed. "You want a raise."

"Only if you think I'm learning."

"Yes, Jyoti. I will tell Suham to pay you six dollars from now on."

I thanked him profusely as I got up and left his office. All the way home, I was beaming. I had no one to share my joy and excitement with. Suddenly, I felt lonely.

The baby was growing big. Whenever I had an appointment with the gynecologist at Gautam's hospital I took the day off, and went with Gautam in the morning. I'd stay with Hetal at her apartment and go to the doctor at the appointment time. Late in the evening, Gautam and I would go home together. At one of these appointments, the doctor did a sonogram and told me I had placenta previa, which meant the placenta was blocking the uterus. This complication could harm the baby as it grew due to increased pressure on the placenta. The doctor asked me to stop working at the seventh month of pregnancy.

I was upset again. I felt fine and the universe was cutting into the already short time I could work. But I didn't have a choice. So after Christmas, I stopped working.

The dark, cold, days seemed even longer as I sat in the apartment looking out the window all day long. I often thought if an artist were to paint a picture of a doctor's wife, it would be a picture of me in the window, looking out.

On a Tuesday morning in February, I saw blood when I went to the bathroom. The doctor told me if that happened, I had to go to the hospital immediately so he could perform a C-section to take the baby out before the placenta caused any distress. I called Gautam and told him about the situation. He rushed home to pick me up and take me to the hospital. Once admitted, the doctor, a big, tall, black man, ordered a sonogram. After getting the results, he told me I was going to have to give a natural birth because the placenta had moved away from the uterus.

"Push," the big, black nurse told me.

"No, he said he was going to operate." I did not cooperate.

"It is better this way. Just listen to me and do what I say."

"And what do you know about childbirth? Do you have any kids?" I was out of control.

"Sweetie, I have four."

Eventually, I did what I was told while Gautam waited outside.

I hated him.

I hated the gynecologist for not sending me to the classes to learn how to push a baby out.

CHAPTER THIRTY-FOUR

1984: PART 1

After a lot of screaming and pushing, much ahead of the due date, our baby girl was born on a cold Thursday morning in February of 1984. She was beautiful with bright shiny eyes. She had no hair at all and her little hands had long fingers. She had a strong, loud cry.

Every time I looked at her, my brain was a hurricane of conflicting thoughts. I realized how vulnerable she was and how much she needed me. And then, I felt guilty for not wanting her in the first place. Then, as if I was talking to her, I'd say, "Hey, don't worry, now you are here. I'll be a good mom to you."

But then I'd wonder, how I was going to do that.

I wondered what my life was going to be like from then on. Would I ever have a career? Would I ever experience a professional life in America and would I be able to ever prove to myself and my dad I was not a failure? Would my dad ever forgive me for doing this selfish thing of having the baby before I'd brought my brother to America? If and when my brother got his green card and came here, how would I support him financially? I was too proud to think Gautam would support my brother's family. And then, I'd circle back to her little face and feel such a powerful need to take care of her. And I told her, "It's you and me from now on. We don't need anyone. We'll be fine."

We didn't know what to name her. Gautam was working so he was in and out of the delivery area. Since she was early, my mother had not arrived from India yet.

The hospital staff kept pushing us to provide a name for the baby girl. In Indian tradition, an astrologer was consulted before naming a newborn. Based on the details of time and place of birth, he would inform the parents of the baby's birth sign and specific letters assigned to it.

Gautam's parents did not believe in astrology. His name and his two brothers' were not based on their astrological signs. My parents had faith in astrology. I watched them refer to a good astrologer for guidance many times. Anytime Dad came across an astrologer with a good reputation for being correct in his predictions or interpretations he would have him look over our horoscopes.

Calling my parents in India to consult an astrologer would take too long. The hospital staff was impatient for the name because they were required to issue a birth certificate.

Not knowing any other Indian we could approach for advice, we decided to name her Bhavna. She had a cheerful and happy face. Bhavna in Indian language means "good feelings" or "gift of God." Both those meanings fit her. Perhaps she was a gift to keep me from my feelings of being lost and to give me a direction for my life.

After delivery, I was transferred to a room on the maternity floor, which I shared with another new mother. I was tired and hungry. The hospital food was not the tastiest, but I had to eat it.

It seemed to me Americans don't know how to eat. There

was no taste to the food, no color, no aroma. The food tray had a cup of fruit in syrup, not palatable at all. Then, there was Jello. Who eats Jello and why? I got by with bread and butter and some steamed green beans that were tasteless without any spices.

Indian food has a colorful mix of spices. Each spice has its own unique taste. Each dish used a special mix the knowledge of which is not written down anywhere. We learn from watching our mothers, who learned from theirs. How much and in what portions spices are added for a dish is oftentimes determined based on the properties of the spice and how it helps the body with digestion and general health. Turmeric gives color to the food but it is tasteless. However, it has anti-inflammatory qualities and hence, used in almost all dishes. Then there is *ajwain* (carom seeds) used only in dishes that can cause gas. Indian cooking is a cultural mix of knowledge about the benefits of various herbs and spices and about the outcomes of their interactions.

The nurse walked into my room holding Bhavna. "Here is your baby, you need to feed her."

"How?" I was too tired and wondered why no one cared for me. Instead, I had to worry about feeding the baby. I didn't know what I was supposed to do and felt guilty about feeling tired and lost.

The nurse was kind and wanted to help. "Breast feed her, I'll teach you. Where is your maternity bra? You are not wearing it?"

"What is a maternity bra?"

"Oh, honey, you don't know anything," she exclaimed with frustration.

Although she was right, her words hurt me. I was sad and angry. I was not angry with the nurse, I was angry because she was right. I remembered when my sister-in-law gave birth to my nephew. So much fuss. All my aunts were there rejoicing and celebrating the occasion. Each of them had brought a nutritious and tasty dish for her. My mom helped with the baby and showed him off to everyone around her.

Derived from the ancient knowledge of herbal medicine and understanding of the human body, there were a few nutritious foods made specifically for the new mother to recover from the physical trauma of childbirth, as well as for the supplementation of nutrition for both the mother and the child through the mother's milk.

One such item they make is from edible gum, a resin extracted from the bark of the Axlewood tree. Available in crystal form as pearly yellowish translucent pieces, it is beneficial for pregnant and postpartum ladies as it strengthens bones and muscles. Eating it helps a new mother's body recover from the childbirth. Round balls are made using ground gum, brown sugar, sesame seeds, valerian root and dried ginger powder, bound with *ghee* (clarified butter). I liked their taste so my sister-in-law had to share them with me.

Memories of the only childbirth I had observed until now and the contrast of what was happening with me made me feel sad and lonely.

My friend, Hetal, who lived in the building across the street, came to see me at the hospital. We talked about how Bhavna surprised us. We were expecting her in April and there she was.

"Do you have baby things at home?" she asked.

"No. I don't know what I will need."

"In America, the pregnant ladies have a baby-shower. Usually someone from family will host it or even friends can host it. Only female friends and relatives are invited and they all come to the party with things that would be useful after the child is born. Usually, one ends up with everything for the baby. I asked Gautam about it, but he did not want me to arrange a shower."

"Why?" I was curious.

"He said he didn't know anybody so there was no one to invite." Hetal replied. "Don't worry, I will go shopping and buy the basics. Have you bought a crib yet?"

"No."

"That's fine. I'll get a bassinet, some clothes for her, baby soap, baby powder, socks and whatever I see in the baby department." She assured me.

"I will tell Gautam to pay you back for all the things you get." I was grateful for her help.

Childbirth is an auspicious occasion in Indian culture. A spiritual event celebrated with *vedic* traditions. A baby shower in India is a religious ceremony taking place at the seventh month of pregnancy during which the good values are imparted to the unborn child, through the chanting of hymns and *shlokas*. The pregnant lady's brother is invited to attend. After the ceremony, he takes his sister home with him, where she stays till the newborn is at least one month old. This allows the new mom's family to fuss over their daughter and take care of her.

Gautam had a large family: two uncles, one aunt, parents, two brothers, and many cousins in California, but no one on the east coast. His family didn't plan for an Indian ceremony in California. They could have had Gautam arrange to send me to California so they could celebrate the anticipated birth of the first grandchild of the family. I felt nobody cared. I didn't matter, neither to Gautam nor to his family. Although I understood the restraints placed upon Gautam's personal, physical, and mental resources due to his work, I couldn't help feeling ignored and neglected. The contrast to the life I had seen in India was painful.

My mother was planning to come based on the expectation the baby was due in April. Also she was not excited about coming because many friends whose daughter or an acquaintance was in America had told her that help was not needed after the first childbirth. Having someone around when the second child was born was more useful, because the first child would need to be cared for. As my brother and his wife worked, she was helping raise their son, who was three now. She did not like that she had to leave them to fend for themselves. But I needed my mom.

Since my mom was not there yet, Gautam called his mother soon after we reached the hospital. She caught a flight from San Francisco and arrived while I was still there. When she arrived he dropped her off at the apartment and returned to work.

He worked on Friday so I didn't see him much. He was aware I would be discharged to go home the next day, but that didn't matter. Residents were literally treated like bonded labor with 12 to 15-hour days.

On Saturday morning, a formidable looking African American nurse came to the room and informed me I was going home. Her actions and mannerism had an urgency that made me panic. I was being rushed out of the room.

"Can I stay here till my husband comes to pick me up?"

"Honey, you can wait in the waiting area. We need the bed."

"Can I call my husband?" I was confused.

I was able to call home and inform my mother-in-law about the discharge.

Before I knew it, I was sitting in the waiting room with my scant belongings in a plastic bag. The baby and I sat facing the entrance and kept staring at it. A few hours went by before Gautam arrived.

I looked up with anticipation every time the sliding door opened, and saw all kinds of people coming into the emergency room. The Bronx Lebanon Hospital, like many big hospital centers, was located in a low socio-economic area of the city. People with no jobs or low paying jobs avoided going to the hospital until the problem became an emergency. This ER was as busy as Grand Central station.

I watched mothers walking in with their injured children, young adults or even tall, dark, middle-aged men walking in with open wounds and cuts from street fights. There were mothers or older sisters with young siblings with a high fever. Ambulances came roaring in with people with gunshot wounds or stab wounds or an elder with acute problems. The people waiting with their family members talked in loud voices, hoping to be heard by the ER staff. It was obvious the hospital was understaffed making the ER remain full at all times.

I kept watching and waiting with my newborn in my lap. On any other day I would have enjoyed watching people, but not today. Today, I was sad.

Eventually, when I saw my husband walk in towards me, I felt relief my wait was ending. However, my relief did not last long.

"I have to make rounds. Let me take you to Hetal's apartment. You can wait there." He was rushing because he was already late for his rounds.

We walked across the street to the apartment building. It was cold. I shivered and checked on the covers over Bhavna as light, fluffy snowflakes came down.

While waiting for Gautam to complete his Saturday rounds, I ran out of diapers. The nurse did not give me enough to last the whole day. Why would she? I was supposed to go home after being discharged.

Even though it was snowing, Hetal walked to the neighborhood store, Red Apple Supermarket, to get a small package of newborn size diapers. The store was on Grand Concourse, about three blocks from the apartment building.

It was evening by the time Gautam was done with rounds on all his patients. He picked me up from Hetal's apartment and we took Bhavna to her new home.

My mother-in-law was waiting for us. She had made dinner with what little groceries we had. It felt good to have home-cooked, tasty Indian food.

She took Bhavna in her arms and said, "I am lucky I have three boys."

I understood exactly what she meant but I was too tired to care. Besides, Gautam was elated to have a daughter, as he didn't have a sister. As for me, gender didn't matter. I was happy to have a healthy, beautiful child.

Exhausted beyond comprehension, I'd never felt this way before. It was like a dark, deep fatigue had seeped into every cell of my body. Everywhere I looked, I saw dark clouds hanging over me. Perhaps, it was the shock I was now responsible for another life. Perhaps it was the dread that, not sure of who I was in this new country, I would fail this responsibility. And yet, Bhavna's needs came before anything I was feeling. My life had changed and would never be the same again.

CHAPTER THIRTY-FIVE
1984-PART 2

My mother's ticket was booked for the end of February. That would have allowed her to become oriented with our life before the baby was born. So, it wasn't long before she arrived. My mother-in-law left soon after.

We arrived a little late to pick her up at JFK.

"I thought you forgot about me," Mom said with an awkward laugh.

Thus began the relationship between Gautam and mom, one of struggled tolerance.

From the time the two families met and Gautam left for the USA after our marriage, less than three weeks, none of us had any time to get to know each other. We were strangers and knew nothing about each other's likes and dislikes, the pet peeves, the personalities, and the sense of humor.

Mom had come far away from her comfort zone and her family, for the first time in her life. By nature she was impatient. With strict discipline and rules, she strived for perfection.

Gautam was overworked, tired and had no control over his

time. His current situation and the fact his family lived by no rules, structure and discipline was a recipe for friction.

Mom and I were both settling down in our new roles. She was getting used to how the switches worked in the opposite way, the stove turned on without a lighter, we could have hot water without having to heat it up on the stove, and there was instant water all day long,

I was learning what it was like to be a mom; the sleepless nights, the diapers, cleaning up with wipes after she pooped, feeding her on regular intervals or at least trying to, giving a bath to this little human being without hurting or drowning her. There was a lot to do all day.

Mom had brought all the nutritional food items they fed a new mom in India. I was happy to have them.

She also brought some stuff babies are given. But Gautam was very firm about not allowing my mom to give those to Bhavna.

"Don't give any of that to Bhavna," he said in a harsh voice. "I don't believe in all that stuff. She might get sick."

One evening, we were having dinner. I asked for the leftover vegetable dish mom had made the day before.

"Ela, don't eat that. Just eat the fresh food I made today."

"Why? You and Gautam are having it."

"Well, it is better for a new mom to avoid a day old food."

Gautam didn't like my mother's remark. "Oh, so it's ok for me to eat old food but not for your daughter?"

In India, it is not a common practice to eat one-day-old food. The only explanation I have for such practice is very few people owned a refrigerator in the old days. Most of the year, temperatures were high and so leftover food spoiled very quickly. No one ate leftovers from lunch for dinner. Cooking fresh meals for lunch and dinner was a norm in India.

Mom tried to explain she had no disrespect for him. But

when Gautam was angry, there was no reasoning with him. I experienced that many times. I told her to stop talking but she felt that logical explanation was necessary. Anger knows no reason because it makes one lose the ability to think. Such interactions with Gautam made my mom very frustrated and sad.

She just couldn't understand my situation. "He is not home much. When he is home, he is angry and tired. He does not play with Bhavna. Why does he talk like this? Is he always this rude?"

"This has been my life. It has not been easy. I hope once his studies are done, it will get better."

"But why can't he talk nicely?"

"I don't know."

"Why do you tolerate such behavior? Even after he is calm he does not apologize."

"What do you expect from me, Mom? Where could I have gone? You arranged this marriage because our horoscopes were a perfect match. Remember?"

"Well, Savita Aunty told us life is perfect in America. Her daughter Mina is very well off. Her husband is very nice. She told me getting a daughter married to a doctor in America was the best idea for her future. When we met Gautam's family they seemed very nice and loving. How much can we learn about them in a short time?"

"That's the point. Isn't it? We can't. No one can. Rushing into this arrangement was not a good idea."

Uncle Raman, my dad's best friend, arranged his daughter, Mina's marriage to an orthopedic surgeon, in the 70's. She often visited India and shared their tales of prosperity and wealth they acquired due to her husband's practice. Having been in the USA for many years, they were obviously well off.

When Mina's brothers didn't do well in school, Uncle

Raman determined his boys were not academically inclined. Mina sponsored both her brothers to emmigrate to America. With their abundant wealth, she and her husband purchased a motel for each of the brothers. They became self-sufficient without having to go to school.

Aunty Savita loved sharing the stories about her daughter with my parents. I wondered if those stories influenced my parents' decision to arrange my marriage.

Mom came with an expectation that my life would be similar to Mina's life. Of course, no one knew anything about a doctor's life during residency.

She felt disappointed about my situation. Having Gautam home only occasionally did not help much, either. They didn't get to know each other at all. For that matter, I was not sure if I knew him well, yet. His behavior was unpredictable, his responses often short and terse.

Once I expressed my frustration to him. "I don't know what to expect from you. Just when I think I have figured out who you are, you react totally opposite of my assumption."

"Unpredictability is a strength," was his short answer.

I put the expectation of a normal relationship and life on hold with the hope things would get better when he was done with residency. Would it ever be?

CHAPTER THIRTY-SIX

1984: PART 3

The tensions between Mom and Gautam were escalating. I was feeling frustrated. We decided Mom did not have to stay the whole six-month term the visa allowed. She left after three months.

Although a correct decision, her departure depressed me. I felt guilty for not having giving her a good time at my home. I failed to establish a balance between her and Gautam. I couldn't convince him to be kinder to her and I couldn't convince her my life was perfect.

I couldn't stop reliving the unpleasant episodes between the two of them and wondering how I could've prevented them. What should I have done and not done to keep peace between the two?

Was it all that bad? Gautam did take us to see the Hindu Temple, "Vrindavan", in West Virginia. Mom enjoyed that trip. We also went to New York City to see the Empire State Building and the World Trade Center.

Postpartum depression and self-loathing, conflicting thoughts, loneliness and the feeling of failure consumed me.

On one Saturday, during the early months of pregnancy, we

visited Chubb Institute, an affiliate of Chubb Insurance Company in Parsippany, New Jersey. Someone had informed us the institute trained potential employees for the insurance company. The candidates were screened and upon qualification, they received an accelerated training in computer programming. I appeared for the screening test and qualified. The course was intense and the recommendation was the student allow at least ten to twelve hours of work between schooling and homework. We decided I would join the course after the baby was born.

Little did we know that going for the course after childbirth would be even more restrictive. Frustrated, Gautam suggested I visit his parents in California.

His mother worked at an Indian restaurant in the evenings. "I am sure there are insurance companies on the west coast that offer training and jobs similar to what Chubb Insurance Company offers. My mom can help with Bhavna while you go to school during the day. We have a big family there. You will feel better."

Reluctantly but also with hope, I flew to California. My in-laws were excited to meet Bhavna. In the first week, dad suggested that Saurabh, Gautam's younger brother, take me to the DMV for a California Identity Card.

"Where are you going?" Mom asked.

"In order to be able to do anything in California, she needs this card. Saurabh will help her with that," Dad replied.

"How long will it be? What am I to do if Bhavna wakes up?"

"Mom, we're going to the DMV and then we'll come right back," I answered. "If she wakes up, the bottles of formula are prepared and stocked in the refrigerator. If the diaper needs to be changed I've put them in the room closet."

"Oh no, I wouldn't know how to do all this. It's been a long time since my youngest grew up."

We assured her we would return as soon as possible and we would not do anything other than apply for the ID card.

Over the next few days, Mom made many such comments that implied she was not going to help with the baby while I took courses at the community college or looked for work.

The disorganized way of life his family lived was not easy for me. I felt lost because of how everybody was living on their own timeline. One person cooked and ate whenever they felt the need. If there was food cooked and ready to eat, the other person would still cook something else and not eat the available food. There was too much waste. Because of this, the refrigerator was full of food, some as old as two weeks. I struggled to find space for Bhavna's formula bottles.

Ajay, the youngest brother's room was full of stuff. There was no floor space to walk around in his room. Many things were dangerous, like the antique knife he had brought from India. I was afraid Bhavna would crawl into his room and get hurt.

"Ajay, you just came home. Why don't you change out of the nice clothes while I serve you dinner." I acted out of old habits from India.

"Even Mom doesn't tell me such things, who are you?" he asked. He was friendly and said it in a jovial way, but I got the message.

It became clear to me I was not going to get much support in that household. They were happy I was there but I did not fit in. I decided to go back to New Jersey, where, if nothing else, I had control over Bhavna's routines and environment.

"You hate my family. They tried, but you just don't like them." Gautam reacted when I returned.

"It's not that. You sent me there so I could work or go to

school. Mom didn't seem to want to help. Then, what was the point of staying there?"

"That's just an excuse. Well, you can't blame me now. I tried."

Why couldn't we understand each other? I was frustrated.

CHAPTER THIRTY-SEVEN
1984: PART 4

After I came back from my in-law's, I was alone with Bhavna for the first time. It took me a week or more to develop my daily routine. Most of the mundane things like going to the bathroom, cooking and cleaning were not difficult. There were many baby products that made it easy for me to take care of Bhavna, things I never saw in India.

This country is quite impressive. The removable basket of the car seat allowed me to take her anywhere in the apartment. The only time I was not comfortable about leaving her was when I needed a shower. I quickly learned to take short showers.

Gautam's life did not change much. Long work hours and sleep deprivation were still constant in our lives. He was excited to have a daughter but couldn't do much about it. He did go to the neighborhood bank to open an account in her name, for her college fund.

Bhavna and I, on the other hand, had many hours to spend together. We were getting used to each other. She was four months old and beginning to seem more like a human being, responding to sounds and toys.

Winter turned to spring, and the days became longer and brighter. With Bhavna in the stroller, I started walking in the parking lot of the apartment complex. Sitting at the corner of two very busy streets, the L-shaped apartment building's parking lot offered much amusement and kept both of us entertained. The sounds of buses and cars buzzing by. The passengers getting off the bus, coming home from work and children going home from school were new and fascinating to watch. For Bhavna it was the movements and sounds. People-watching encouraged me to go for our daily walks.

One early evening, I spotted an elderly lady, sitting on the steps of her ground floor apartment. She had a round and happy face, white curly hair and wore a floral piece of clothing, which had short sleeves, snap down buttons in the front joining the two sides of the clothing with two pockets in the front. Her smile displayed her beautiful teeth and I felt she had a warm heart. She was looking inside the open door and talking with someone.

When we were closer to her apartment, she exclaimed, "What a beautiful baby! Are you new to the complex? What number is your apartment?"

As we strolled over to where she sat, she asked, "What is your name?"

"Jyotsana," I replied.

"Say that again."

I repeated my name many times until she responded with frustration. "I'm going to call you Jo. I am Addy."

"That's ok," I replied and tested her patience with Bhavna's name.

"And I'll call her baby," she decided promptly. "Well, sit down. We'll watch the baby together."

She pointed to the man sitting inside, by the open door and said, "This is my husband, Tom."

Tom had a round, pale face and white hair. He had droopy eyes and drank a lot of coffee. He informed me, "We both retired from our jobs with the United States Post Office."

I did not know how to address Addy and her husband. Although she told me her name, I could not bring myself to call her Addy. In India, people our parents' age are addressed as Uncle and Aunty, and those close to grandparents' age are our "Ba" and "Dada." Young men older than me get "bhai" attached to their name and older girls get "ben."

How could I address them as just Addy and Tom? It should be Addy Auntie and Tom Uncle. Why do people in America show no respect for older people? Or is it that addressing an older person by their name is not considered disrespectful? Anyway, I felt awkward so I decided to start a conversation without ever saying their names.

"Would you like some coffee?" she asked.

Not having developed the taste for bitter black coffee, I politely refused.

We began learning things about each other. She shared they could not have children. I too, felt comfortable enough with Addy, that I voiced my frustrations with her. Going for strolls in the parking lot and hanging out with Addy and Tom added a happy routine to my lonely life.

Addy often made pound cake. "Would you like a piece? I made it myself; I always do because I don't like store bought cakes."

"Yes," I said, never had a pound cake, let alone a homemade one.

I loved it. It was moist and sweet and I felt like I could live my entire life just eating pound cake, no other food item necessary.

Addy's pound cake was a delicious addition to our strolls.

When summer turned into fall and then winter, our

parking lot meetings came to a stop. I had to visit Addy and Tom inside their apartment. It was not the same, but Bhavna was close to ten months old and enjoyed playing with colorful toys that made sounds when she finished stacking or pushed a button.

"Isn't her birthday coming soon?" Addy asked me.

"Yes, on February 23rd she will be one year old." I responded excitedly.

"What's the plan? Are you having a birthday party for her?"

"I don't know. Gautam and I have not thought about it. I'll talk to him."

In the days that followed I brought up Bhavna's birthday with Gautam. We didn't have many friends and since I had not been to a birthday party in America, I didn't know how to plan one. We talked about a few things, but there was not enough time to finish conversations.

In India, birthdays were not a big deal. Mom would make a favorite dessert or we would go out for dinner. Often a nice dinner at home followed by ice cream made for a happy celebration.

One evening Gautam informed me, "We will have Bhavna's birthday party at Chuck -E- Cheese. I have told a few of my colleagues to come there with their wife."

"But I don't know them." I felt a little awkward about meeting his colleagues for the first time at our daughter's birthday party.

"It's ok, they will bring their wives. It'll be alright."

"Can I invite Addy?"

"Sure. She is your friend."

Addy helped me order a cake.

At the party I felt uncomfortable and lost. Gautam introduced me to his friends, but I couldn't spend much time with anyone because of Bhavna. She wanted to keep running and following other kids in the restaurant. I gave her a balloon to hold and play with but she quickly learned that if she let it go, she could run to catch it. Eventually, I had to have her sit on a table, where Addy and I kept her busy. Meanwhile, Gautam and his co-residents stayed busy eating pizza and talking about the upcoming graduation and plans after that.

At another table, women who seemed familiar with each other were chatting.

Later, everybody gathered around the cake and sang the traditional "Happy Birthday" song. Then we went home.

"Did you enjoy the party?" Gautam asked.

"I didn't know anyone. You were busy talking business. The women were nice but I didn't have much time to get to know them because I was with Bhavna the whole time. Thank God, Addy was there to keep me company."

He defended himself. "Why do you complain? We didn't know what to do about her birthday so I came up with this plan."

I didn't want to argue.

Bhavna was growing fast. I enjoyed watching her change every day. I observed that when I left her near the couch she started to cry. I didn't think she felt insecure because she could watch me going around in the apartment. But then, why was she crying? I observed every time she was crying she was looking at my feet.

"Do you want to walk?" I asked her while holding her little hands and helped her step towards me. She was ecstatic, giggled happily, with a big smile as she tried to walk. Mystery solved.

CHAPTER THIRTY-EIGHT

1985- PART 1

One day we ran into an Indian couple. They told us the lady's mom, my mother's age, was looking for a baby-sitting job. Gautam suggested I look for a job, have this lady, Induben, come to our apartment, and take care of Bhavna.

I liked the idea very much. Somehow, having an Indian babysitter seemed more acceptable. I found a store manager's position at an electronic parts store, Nidisco. John, a man older than my dad, owned the store, from which he sold every electronic part needed for repair of small gadgets, personal and professional.

I didn't know anything about electronic items but John offered me the position as long as I was willing to answer phones and call customers for collecting on unpaid bills.

I was delighted but now I needed a way to get to work. Since we both needed cars, Gautam suggested we sell the Malibu and purchase two smaller cars for us. I settled on a new Nissan Stanza and my husband bought a used Toyota Corolla. Now, I could get to work on my own.

At work, Larry, the only other employee in the store, was very knowledgeable about all the products. He was quiet and took care of the walk-in customers as well as shipping out packages for the phone orders. Until I was hired, he never had time to do the things that were not related to ordering and selling products. I organized the store's records, classified the filing by customers and vendors, and was not afraid to call and ask for money. John was impressed and pleased with my work.

The store was in Hackensack, not too far from Little Ferry. After work I drove home and took Induben to her son's home, as she did not drive.

I tried to make most of the dinner in the morning before leaving for work. After dropping off Induben, I finished the rest of the cooking, which mostly consisted of making "roti," the Indian flat bread.

As Gautam was not home much, Bhavna did not think of him as a family member and often cried when she saw him in the apartment. The fact he did not offer to play with her while I finished making dinner did not help much. Very tired he did not seem to have energy and desire to handle a baby that did not recognize him. He watched television with a loud volume. Every evening, Bhavna crawled into the kitchen and sat by my feet while I cooked.

Waking up early, cooking, making sure everything was ready for Induben, working all day and coming home to more chores was exhausting. I felt as though Bhavna should have at least one parent dedicated to her upbringing. I quit working.

John was disappointed but understood.

Bored at home again, I was depressed and sad. Gautam did not understand how I felt. No matter how much I tried to explain, he did not get it. He assumed too much and didn't let me talk. Solitude kept the disappointments from my mother's visit alive.

One can let go of the past and move on if the situation changes but if similar experiences keep repeating, how can one forget the past? Thinking about the same things over and over, keeps the emotions alive and sometimes even growing, like a diabetic foot ulcer.

Soon, it was spring again. I restarted our parking lot walks. This time, though, I had to let her out of the stroller every now and then. Otherwise, she was not going to allow me to have any conversations with Addy.

"My husband will be finishing his residency this June. He said there would be a graduation ceremony," I shared with Addy one evening.

"Are you going?"

"Am I allowed to go?"

"Of course. It's a very special occasion for both of you."

"I don't know. He didn't say anything. Maybe he doesn't know either, or maybe he thinks babies can't go and we have no one to watch her." I tried to explain to myself more than to Addy.

"Oh no, Jo, you have to go. I'll watch the baby." She insisted. "Buy yourself a dress, get your hair done and go with him."

"Really?"

"Yes."

In the days that followed, I discussed graduation with Gautam. He was happy Addy offered to watch Bhavna while I attended his graduation.

I asked Addy, "Where do I go to get my hair done?

"There is a hairdresser who works out of her apartment, across the street."

Addy had answers for every question. She watched Bhavna while I made a visit to the hairdresser. After one look at my long, thick hair that reached below my waist, the hairdresser exclaimed, "what can I do with your hair? It is long and heavy so it won't hold a curl. You want me to cut it short and then style it?"

I didn't understand what the term "style" meant, but I was not going to let her cut my hair.

When I refused, she humored me, "I'll do something, don't worry." She gave me an appointment.

Thanks to Addy, I was able to dress up and get my hair styled for the first time in America.

My hair looked beautiful. The hairdresser used an electric instrument that caught a strand of hair between two heated steel plates and rolled it up towards the scalp, while spraying something from an aerosol can. When she let go after a few seconds, the strand was curly. She repeated the process until all my hair was curly and bouncy from the ends. Then, she tried to find shorter hair growing towards the front of my face and curled them.

"Your hair is heavy so I am using a lot of spray. Hopefully, the curl will last through the evening." She explained to me. "You don't have bangs in the front so the shorter hair I have curled in the front will have to sit sideways for a nice look." She continued, "Don't touch your hair until the party is over, ok."

My hair looked pretty from afar but it felt stiff to touch. I didn't like that feel. But I followed her instructions as I told myself, "This is how these people do to their hair every day. You will tolerate it for one evening."

The graduation event didn't seem as formal as I thought. It was held for only the five general surgery graduates. The department of surgery staff and some doctors who trained the five graduates were also present. I recognized some of the staff members from my volunteer days. We did not stay long because Gautam was tired and I was worried about Bhavna.

. . .

Gautam was not sure about our future. How could he be? The program was not allowing the residents any time to think, let alone plan for a life after residency. He was interested in vascular surgery and wanted to apply for a fellowship to learn more. But there was no opportunity during his fourth year to apply in a timely manner.

Bhavna's birth and my mother's subsequent visit, along with the burdens of residency, affected our life in ways we did not even understand.

One day, he gave me a list of fellowship programs all over the United States. I prepared a cover letter and his resume on his IBM Selectric typewriter. He made copies of both documents. During the week, I addressed the envelopes and mailed them out. I don't think I mailed all of them before he broke the news about his decision.

His anxiety about supporting his family and his lack of faith, either in himself or the system, made him impatient. So, when an Air Force Recruiting Officer showed up at the hospital he thought his prayers were answered. He made a quick decision to join the Air Force, on the condition he would be stationed in California.

He felt many of our problems would disappear once we were in a nurturing, safe environment, surrounded by his parents, uncles, aunts, and cousins.

I was not so optimistic. Since I came to the USA, none of his family members had tried to connect with me. Even when Bhavna was born, there were no phone calls congratulating us. I just didn't feel that sense of family from anyone.

My family was not perfect. No one's is. But there were signs of life there, arguments among my parents and their siblings and yet rushing to be available during emergencies.

There was jealousy, there was anger, and there was also laughter and joy at family gatherings for special festivals. I remember all of us helping Mom cook a feast for my dad's sisters when they came every year to tie the sacred thread of protection around my dad's wrist on *Raksha Bandhan*. No matter what the emotion, there were signs of life, of being human, of belonging to a larger group. That feeling was absent in his family and to blame the lack of proximity for the lack of connection was like saying the sun did not rise just because it was behind the clouds.

"I joined the U.S Air Force," Gautam excitedly informed me as a matter of fact. "We are going to California."

He would finish his residency at the end of June 1985. We had many conversations about his career plans.

He wanted to be a vascular surgeon. We were in the process of applying for a fellowship. I typed his resume to send with fellowship applications. I was stuffing the envelopes to mail to programs all over the country. The department of surgery where he was doing his residency, Bronx Lebanon Hospital, also offered him a job.

The news about moving to California came as a total surprise. "What?" I blurted out in disbelief.

"Yeah. The Air Force will help us move." He was excited. "I will have the rank of a Captain because of my level of education. Even better, they promised to place us on a base in California. We will be closer to the family."

He was going on as if I had been involved in this decision.

"When did you decide? Are we discussing this or did you already sign the papers? What about the fellowship? Don't you want to work in a familiar place, at the same hospital?"

"I will never get accepted for a vascular fellowship. Some of the specialty residencies have few positions and they are mostly reserved for white candidates."

"But they admitted you to the residency program. Why do you feel that way?"

"I already signed a contract. It's done. I want to get out of New York. The officer will come and explain the moving process." He had made up his mind and signed the papers while I was stuffing envelopes.

A week later, an officer came to our apartment. He explained the movers would come on an agreed date, pack everything in boxes and store all our belongings in storage until we were ready to have it brought to us at our new home. Gautam would be going to San Antonio, Texas for in-processing into the United States Air Force and receive the Red-flag training.

Then, the officer revealed, without even the slightest hesitation, that Gautam would be working at Fairchild Air Force Base in Washington.

Gautam turned pale. "Oh no, I was promised a base in California. This is not right."

The officer was calm. "Yes, Sir, but upon further audit of human resources, there is no opening in California. You can request a posting in California when you are about to end your first term of service."

This was not acceptable to me. If the Air Force is already going back on its promises, I doubted everything else they promised would come true. "Let's cancel. We don't have to do this."

"Too late, Ma'am. The documents have been signed."

CHAPTER THIRTY-NINE

NEW JERSEY / SAN FRANCISCO 1985-PART 2

I wished Gautam had asked me before making this life changing decision. But it was too late. All I could do now was hope he was right and once we were in California. There, I would feel more integrated in his family and have the sense of security I hungered for.

I also felt tired at the thought of having to change our lives again. It was as if I was on the run, always rushed. First I rushed to settle down in the US, then rushed to learn to be a mom, and now before I felt confident and settled, I was going to have to rush to move and start over.

Contrary to their promise, the Air Force did not station us in California. How was Spokane, Washington any different than New York in the opportunity to connect with the family?

We started packing for the move. It was difficult because Bhavna, sixteen months old now, was getting into everything that needed to be packed. It was a great relief when the Air Force movers showed up, packed and loaded the truck. They took all our belongings to a military storage facility. We were relieved to find out we didn't have to worry about renting a place near the base for the movers to deliver our belongings. They would deliver everything when we were ready to move into the base housing in July.

We decided to sell the Toyota and have the Nissan transported through a company that found people wanting to travel cross-country but did not have their own car. The three of us flew to San Francisco. It was our first flight with Bhavna. I was nervous but it worked out fine. She was a friendly baby and was not afraid of too many people in small spaces.

Addy and I spent many hours together in the parking lot until we left for the west coast. She watched as we drove away. Bhavna kept looking back and waving at her, and she back at her, till the road turned.

Driving towards the airport, I kept wondering if I would ever see Addy again. Would I find a friend like her? I'd have to start over one more time. As for Addy, she was old. Who will be there for her?

Gautam's parents came to the airport to receive us. There was an excitement about seeing Bhavna again after almost a year. We were going to live with them until Gautam's return from Texas, where he would be going for training, then drive to Fairchild Air Force Base, outside Spokane, Washington.

From my past experience with Gautam's family, I was not too excited about staying with them for three weeks.

His family's lifestyle and culture were very different from mine. We had regular meal times. They ate while walking around all day long. We thought twice before spending money. They did not think at all. We had a place for everything and everything was put back in its place. They never put anything where it belonged. Sometimes you could find toothpaste in the refrigerator and a cooking utensil in the bedroom. Everyone cooked whatever he or she felt like eating, whenever they wanted to eat. The cooked food sat in the refrigerator for a long time until there was no space, then everything got thrown out.

Once, when I saw there was no space to put Bhavna's baby food and formula bottles in the refrigerator, I recruited Gautam to help me with it.

He didn't understand my nervousness but helped me anyway. Together we threw away molding food containers, rearranged the fresh food, wiped down everything inside the fridge and made room for Bhavna's food.

Late at night, when his mom came home from her restaurant job, she instantly inquired, "Who touched my things in the refrigerator?"

"We did. There was a lot of rotting food in it. It's much cleaner now, right?" Gautam answered.

I dared not open my mouth. Whenever I did something differently than her, even if it was the right thing, she assumed I was doing it to spite her. For example, I didn't like to eat pickled mango because it is loaded with salt and oil. My mother, the health fanatic, did not support the idea of eating pickles, except occasionally with certain foods, as a garnish or dip. Gautam's mother, on the other hand, considered pickles to be the main dish. She was proud that every summer in India she used to make a huge quantity but would have nothing left before the next mango season arrived.

"Can I give you some pickles?" She asked at every meal, knowing fully well what my answer would be. "I don't know why you won't eat it." She could not comprehend the idea someone wouldn't like what she liked.

"Why did you clean the refrigerator? Don't you think if you are at someone's home and clean their place, they would feel as if you were telling them they are dirty people?"

Here we go, I thought.

CHAPTER FORTY

SAN FRANCISCO/ARKANSAS 1985: PART 3

As if the universe were listening, just as I stressed about having to stay with Gautam's parents while he went to Texas for his training, my friend, Hetal from the Bronx, called.

A year before us, when her husband's residency finished they had moved away from the Bronx to Hot Springs, Arkansas.

My friend called me at my in-law's home to see how we did with the move. I shared the latest and ended with my unhappiness about having to stay with Gautam's family for three weeks during his training.

"Why don't you come here?" she suggested

"How? I don't think they'd like that. It would be rude."

Hetal did not have children yet, but her sister's kids, eight-year-old, Neil, and five-year-old, Shital, used to visit her during summer vacation.

"Why not? Neil and Shital will have fun playing with Bhavna. Gautambhai can drop you off when he comes to Texas for training."

Not quite fluent about the map of the USA, I was surprised at her suggestion.

"No. It would be too much. Why would he go out of his way to do that?"

"It's not that far. He can drop you off and then go to San Antonio."

I shared my phone conversation with Gautam.

He was quick to respond. "Sure, I can do that."

"Isn't it far?"

"Let's look at the map," he suggested while opening up the big Rand McNally map book.

It seemed far to me, but he didn't mind. It was quickly decided I was going to Arkansas. Sometimes, I didn't know what to think about him. When I felt he would be upset, he was the most amicable. Other times when I thought nothing about something, he made a big deal about it. I was still learning.

We drove to Arkansas. It was a long drive. We had to stay overnight three times and had to stop often to let Bhavna run around freely.

I enjoyed seeing the vast expanse of the land with highways going through nothingness for long patches. I was surprised to see how much the inland states we drove through had no settlements, buildings, or signs of civilization, and yet there were great highways. At sunset, we saw the sun going down at the end of the road from our car. It looked like the old cowboy movies I used to watch on the stolen HBO in the Bronx. Well, all that wasn't made up, after all.

We reached Hot Springs in the evening. Hetal and her husband, Rajesh, were excited to see us after one year. We had dinner with them. Indian food for dinner after three days was very soothing.

Neil and Shital took charge of Bhavna, while Hetal and I talked about life in Hot Springs and Gautam and Rajesh sat in the family room, talking about life after residency.

In the morning, Gautam drove away to San Antonio, Texas.

Three weeks with a normal family was just what I needed. Three meals a day, at regular times, going out for fun with kids in the early evening, and talking about real concerns and hopes. I couldn't ask for more.

Bhavna, quickly became a fun toy for Neil and Shital. The house had two stories with a wide staircase covered with carpet. She climbed the stairs and then slid down, bumping her diaper-covered behind, laughing loudly. I think the effect of the bumps on her laughing voice was amusing to her. It was the first time I saw her playing with older kids and the way the three played and interacted was a treat to watch.

Three weeks passed in a blink of an eye and Gautam was there to pick us up. He looked slim and fit. On our drive back, he described the training he went through. He had to cross a long distance between two hills using a rope. And then, jump in the mud and keep going forward. He had to learn to prepare meals from dehydrated food packets just like the soldiers. It was tough, but he enjoyed it and believed he was ready for war.

We did not have much time together after we reached his parents' home, on July 10th. He had to report for duty on July 19, 1985.

CHAPTER FORTY-ONE
SPOKANE, WA 1985: PART 4

Fairchild Air Force Base

A few days after we returned from Texas, we packed up and left for Spokane. The Air Force advised Gautam we should stay in the Baghdad Motel, right outside the base, in a little town called Airway Heights. This time, driving with a small child did not seem so daunting after our long trip to Texas and back. We understood how long to drive before stopping to give Bhavna a break from the restraint of the car seat. She was still unhappy about her plight, but it was as if her little brain had learned the pattern.

The instructions from the Air Force were detailed. I was impressed about how the entire process was handled. I began to understand that, unlike in India, everything ran smoothly in the US because there a well-defined system and everybody was trained to follow it.

We checked into the Baghdad Motel. Tired, we fell asleep right away. Gautam had to report to the base in the morning.

When I awoke, I looked at the room and knew it was an old establishment that had seen a lot of traffic. The room contained a kitchenette with a gas stovetop that was scratched up from many years of cleaning and scrubbing. The room smelled of a mixture of foods, mostly meat, like Burger King or MacDonald's.

The sheets were faded and the bed covers showed signs of age on the edges. The furniture complained loudly about the abuse it had endured. Fortunately, the entire motel had only one row of rooms. Most of the day, I felt safe leaving the door open and letting in the fresh air.

One thing good about Gautam's mom was that her intense fear of hunger made her pack excessive amounts of food for travel. For once, it was a good thing. We had enough food to last for the day. The dry snacks, spicy crunchy *pooris*, lasted even longer. Made from *maida*, bleached refined white flour, salt, red ground pepper, turmeric, and whole cumin seeds, these small round deep fried crunchy bread have provided solace to many generations of Gujarati travelers.

After a full day of in-processing, the term used by the Air Force for a new recruit's orientation, Gautam came back to us in the evening bearing bad news. There was no vacancy in base housing and we'd have to stay in the Baghdad Motel for a few more days. How many? We would be informed later.

Deciding to settle in, we went grocery shopping and stocked up on the basics: milk, eggs, bread, fruits, laundry detergent, dish soap and paper plates.

The routine of our Air Force life had started. Gautam went to the base in the morning and Bhavna and I walked a little, watched TV and napped since there was not much else to do.

On the third day, after Gautam left for work, Bhavna started having diarrhea. She could not keep anything down and was getting dehydrated. Towards the early evening, she was difficult to manage. I walked around with her in my arms. Her toys, favorite TV shows, or books didn't appease her because of her sore and irritated bottom. Even Mickey Mouse failed to bring a smile during her favorite Mousercise show. I couldn't wait for Gautam to get back to us.

He arrived to find us in distress and immediately drove to the only pharmacy and brought back over the counter (OTC) antidiarrheal and Pedialyte to help with the electrolytes. We hoped she would get a break from bouts of diarrhea in a few hours.

However, nothing changed except Bhavna was getting more irritable and weaker. On the second day, he came home and found the previous day's treatment plan had not worked. He was afraid she might have Giardiasis.

"What is that?

His face full of worry, he responded, "Let's go to the base hospital and have a pediatrician take a look."

Gautam stopped the car at the front gate which looked similar to the toll stations on the highways of New Jersey. The gatekeeper checked his military identification and allowed us to enter. I realized this must be one of the in-processing activities Gautam did in the last two days.

I stepped foot on a United States Air Force Base for the first time. It was a feeling I could neither describe nor enjoy because of the circumstances, but the event and its special significance was not lost on me.

We drove straight to the hospital, Bhavna still uneasy and looking sad.

The emergency room checked us in. Bhavna and I were not in the system yet, but it did not seem to pose a problem because they all knew of a new surgeon coming to the base.

The emergency room nurse called for a pediatrician, who after listening to the history of Bhavna's symptoms, prescribed Flagyl, an antimicrobial. We were informed the pharmacy was inside the hospital, making it easy for us since we knew nothing about the layout of the base, yet.

The medication worked. After two doses Bhavna's symptoms began to ease. In a few more days, we were back to walking around the motel, which was a good thing because Gautam was told we may not be able to get into base housing for another two and a half weeks.

CHAPTER FORTY-TWO

1985: PART 5

It was over a month before we were assigned housing on the base. Our house stood on a street beyond which was a wide-open space, as if the Air Force people had a plan for it, but they forgot. Facing the street and the open field, on the right, the housing area merged with the main road coming from the main entrance. To the left, the street ended with a small playground, a little merry-go-round, slide, a couple of swings, and lots of dirt.

"Believe me, this is not America," Crystal, my new friend on the base quipped. She had an assurance that only someone who had lived inside and outside of the base could give.

Crystal's comment perplexed me. The nurse in the Bronx hospital said New York was not America. If neither New York nor the Air Force Base were America then where was it?

I met Crystal at the daycare center where I signed Bhavna up for three hours a day. Her two daughters, one Bhavna's age and one younger, also attended the same day care.

Crystal, an African American from Georgia, was a proud woman. Her husband was a pilot. She felt she needed to go the extra mile to prove as black Americans, they deserved to be part of an elite society. I did not understand her perspective and questioned her many times. But she didn't think I'd understand.

She ironed all her clothes, even her daughters' daily wear. She and her two girls dressed well. Always trying to fit in, she drove a Volvo Station Wagon.

I was unaware of the ideas and thoughts she expressed. I wished she were not in so much emotional pain. I liked her. I found her accent interesting and loved to listen to her talk. She, on the other hand, loved listening to Bhavna. "Girl, she cracks me up. Look at her talk like a grandma," she'd say with her southern accent.

One day at a time, we finally settled on the base. Gautam seemed relaxed. He no longer had to work two or three days at a stretch without sleep. The hospital culture was laid back compared to the constant flow of patients in the Bronx. If the emergency room in New York was Grand Central Station, the Emergency Room on the base was like an old railroad station portrayed in movies about the wild West days in California. The reduced workload gave him time to study for the Surgery Board Exam.

Bhavna and I made short trips to various places on the base to acquaint ourselves with its services and facilities. Crystal advised me groceries could be bought at the Commissary, a store all military bases had where families could shop at lower prices than similar stores off base. Contrary to the private retail industry that could mark up the prices of groceries as they saw fit, the base commissaries charged only five percent over the cost of goods. All I needed was my military ID to take advantage of the discounted prices.

Bhavna and I had a routine in our life. Wake up and go to school, come home and try to take a nap, and then in the early evening, go to the park at the end of the street.

Very few Indian people joined the Air Force, so needless to say, there were no Indian families on the Base. Gautam explained most physicians in the armed services were there because the US government paid for their medical school education. They were obligated to work in the military. A majority of Indian doctors had come to the US after finishing their medical school education in India, then directly entered the residency program. They did not owe the military. People of Indian origin in the military were a rarity.

There was a Morale, Welfare and Recreation (MWR) building, commonly called the Rec Center, on the base. The building housed classes for arts and crafts, plus a bowling alley, library, pool, youth center, daycare center, and a gym. They offered a ceramics class where they even had a kiln to put the finished clay products to dry and harden into perfect shapes.

I decided to join the ceramics class. I surprised myself because I never thought I was crafty. In the past, I did not have the patience needed to start and finish a craft project such as embroidery, artwork with a glue gun, or painting.

When my cousin, Hema, came to spend summer vacations at our home my mom hoped I'd become more artistic and creative like her. "Hema, make that picture of Lord Krishna with sequins and beads with Ela. She will not do it on her own. She needs to learn."

Grudgingly, I finished the project using pink, turquoise, and gold sequins. I used white beads for Krishna's garland. Hema glued half of them just to make sure it turned out perfectly.

My mother was so pleased with the outcome she framed the finished picture of Lord Krishna and hung it on the wall.

. . .

Much to my surprise, I enjoyed ceramics. It was quite possible doing anything other than playing with Bhavna may have made ceramics tolerable. The first piece I made was a small horse with a mother-of-pearl finish. When it came out of the kiln, I was proud.

Later, I made a figure of a duck sitting on a rock. Painting it after it came out of the kiln, I was impressed I had the patience. Pleased with the finished product, I decided to give it to my dad when I visited knowing he'd be surprised and proud.

The thought I'd wasted my education never left me. I could hear my parents say, "We didn't spend our scant resources for your education so you could sit at home and do nothing. You still have to make sure you can sponsor your brother to come to the US."

Deep in the back of my brain, the words were like an itch I'd get from poison ivy. I couldn't stop scratching.

I thought about going to college, but Washington State University was in Pullman, eighty-five miles away. Because of the harsh and long winters, the distance would seem even longer, plus, I was not comfortable driving in unpredictable weather. Gautam's work, though less grueling, was still filled with uncertainty. I could not plan anything that required me to be somewhere on a regular schedule or be dependent on him.

"Ela, how about mail order courses?" Gautam suggested once.

"For what?" I wondered what he meant.

"Well, you can learn whatever you want. They will send you study material and you take the test and mail it back to them." He explained, "it's one way of getting more education."

I agreed with Gautam and explored the courses I could take. After a few days, I decided I would love to learn about how to prepare tax returns. I had seen ads by H&R Block who were looking for people to work during tax season to help them with the increased workload. I thought if I could take a tax preparation course I could work with H&R Block. I enrolled in a mail order course and received the books and study materials very soon.

I loved learning about the Federal Internal Revenue Service, State income tax, form 1040, payroll taxes, standard deductions, and itemized deductions. All this was exciting to me. I finished before the expected graduation date. I felt I was ready to prepare tax returns. But for whom?

CHAPTER FORTY-THREE

"Ela, why don't you go to the administration office and ask about volunteering?" Gautam suggested.

The next morning, after dropping Bhavna off at the day care center, I drove straight to the administration building, located near the entrance gate.

Inside the building was a waiting room where a young lady in uniform stood behind a counter to help whoever needed it. Beyond that, were a few office spaces with scant furnishings, a desk and a chair.

"Hi, I want to volunteer," I told the lady behind the counter.

She summoned a young, handsome man in uniform and repeated what I had said.

"Ma'am, you want to volunteer on the base?"

"Yes."

"What kind of work would you like to do?"

"Is there an accounting office that offers free services to the base residents?" I wasn't sure if I made sense to them because I couldn't explain what I wanted to say.

The two looked at each other for a few seconds before the

young man said, "I don't believe they've ever had volunteers in the accounting office. Most volunteers help out at the Recreation Center, or the stores."

"The base doesn't offer help with tax returns?" I asked as if the base should be doing so.

Again, they looked at each other. "No ma'am, I don't believe they provide that kind of service here. Would you like to volunteer to prepare free tax returns for our base residents?" the handsome fellow asked.

I was terrified and yet delighted to hear him say those words. "Yes, I would."

"Ma'am, are you an accountant? I mean, are you qualified to prepare tax returns?" the young staff member asked me.

"Yes," I replied with confidence. "I have an MBA from India. I recently took a course in tax law and tax preparation."

"It would be helpful if you provided me with your resume and the completion certificate of the course you mentioned." He was so polite.

He explained this was something that had never been done before so he'd have to check with higher-level staff members and needed time to do so. He promised he'd call me.

I left the building hopeful and glad I'd made an effort.

It had been three days since I dropped off the resume and a copy of the certificate. I had not heard from the administration office.

When Gautam noticed my impatience, he reminded me the Air Force was a bureaucracy where everything required filling out request forms that would travel through a series of people at different levels of hierarchy. Then someone with authority to approve such requests would review it and make a decision. In short, he advised me to be patient.

Gautam was speaking from experience. He was already showing signs of frustration. Young and recently graduated, he was bored with the scarce work he was doing at the hospital. The number of hours he worked at the base hospital was less than half of what he had worked in the Bronx.

He was working under another surgeon who was more than twice his age and had long passed the phase of life where he felt excited about doing more operations and trying new techniques. Gautam's enthusiasm was often met with a cold shoulder. If there was ever any interest in something he suggested, the delays caused due to tedious and lengthy paperwork irritated him.

After a week, I received a phone call from the administration office asking me to be ready to work the next day. I was overjoyed. Then panic set in.

Will I be able to do the tax returns? Do I have enough training? What if I mess up and someone doesn't get a refund? What did I get myself into?

I showed up at the administration office at 8:30 am. The front desk attendants welcomed me. They took me to one of the rooms I had seen on my last visit. It was a corner cubicle with a desk, one chair behind the desk and two in front, for the visitors.

"This is your desk. We will make appointments for the employees who want to take advantage of your service. Let us know if there is anything else you need."

Apparently, the administration office had let the base employees know a free tax preparation service was available and had already scheduled someone at 9:00 am.

There was no going back for me. I was either going to do a good job with the taxes or apologize for not knowing what I was doing.

The first client, a young man, arrived. He showed me his paycheck stubs and the W-4 he had received from the Air Force. I went over the deductions from his paychecks, both federal and state. I asked him about the items on page two of Form 1040, trying to figure out if he had spent more in the categories under the section labeled Itemized Deductions to see if the total added up to more than the standard deduction IRS allowed. I advised him his return would be ready in a day or two and someone would let him know.

Profusely thanking me, he left. I took a deep breath. It felt as if I was in an alternate reality. *Was I really sitting in "my" office? Did I really have assistants who made appointments for clients to see me?*

Most of the people who came for help were young employees who joined the Air Force after high school or two-years of college. Their lives had not become complicated yet; but their fear of doing something wrong or losing out on a tax refund was palpable.

I prepared many tax returns in the 1986 tax season, and was proud I could help twenty people. I hoped I'd be able to do more the following year.

CHAPTER FORTY-FOUR

1985-87: PART 1

During his surgery training in New York, Gautam was impatient, agitated and preoccupied. Only five out of twenty students would graduate as general surgeons. The competition was cutthroat. No behavior was off-limits for survival. The other residents in the program had more familiarity with the hospital systems and employees because they started a month before him. They'd arrange their time off just before the annual in-service exam so Gautam would end up taking emergency room calls and have no time to study. Often, they didn't make him aware of the specific way an attending surgeon liked things done. Then sent Gautam off to assist the attending. He got in trouble because he didn't know what was expected of him.

Amidst such tough times, his parents insisted he go to India with them to have his marriage arranged. They did not understand, and did not want to understand what he was going through. Four months later, I was living with him. Our relationship started under tense circumstances.

It was hard to have a conversation with him. I felt as if I was in his way. He didn't need me. It was difficult for me to grasp the magnitude of his frustration, bothering him even more. Once, when I didn't want to go with some of his colleagues, he was angry. I explained, "I think the doctors are all very arrogant and don't like talking about anything other than their work and hospital."

"You are saying that because you are jealous of me. I know you think your brother deserved to be where I am, so you are angry at me."

His comment upset me. He didn't want to understand what I needed and was quick to assume something totally unrelated. I regretted having shared anything about my life before we met.

We had many such conversations where I realized he was not my friend. We had no chance to develop friendship and trust.

My friend, Addy, used to say we needed counseling. I did not know what she meant but if it needed his time, we couldn't have done it. I tried hard to have faith and believed he'd be one of the five and then life would get better.

In the Air Force, there was no fear of not making it through the residency, no stress of eighty-hour weeks, and not much sleep deprivation. Yet, as we progressed in our lives on the base I noticed his agitation and frustration returning.

This time it was his boss and, surprisingly, not enough work. It bothered him the base hospital did not offer endoscopy services. He wanted to do more upper endoscopies. He worked hard to convince the senior doctor that the hospital needed to provide those services and then worked even harder to get the department up and running.

Again, I was lost. I couldn't understand him, and he couldn't understand me. It was as if we needed interpreters.

I spent a lot of time with Bhavna. I developed a daily routine, with time allotted to various activities and toys. The time she spent at daycare were the few hours I had to myself. The daily schedule did not include Gautam.

Watching Bhavna interacting with other children at the daycare center made me realize she needed a brother or a sister to play with.

I shared my thoughts with Gautam. He agreed. We decided to have another child.

Soon, I was pregnant.

I called his mother. "We are going to have another baby."

"Isn't that too soon? Bhavna is only two and a half years old. I didn't have a second child for six years after Gautam was born."

"There's a difference in our situations. Gautam had cousins to play with. You had families on both sides that provided support. We are alone here. I feel Bhavna needs company. The two can grow up together. I am spending a lot of time alone with Bhavna. If I have a second child, I can raise them both together."

"Oh, well, do what you want. I'll see if I can come to help when you are ready to deliver. You'll need someone to care for Bhavna at home when you are in the hospital. If she were grown up, she would stay by herself."

"It's ok Mom. We'll figure it out."

I called my mom in India to give her the news.

"Your sister-in-law is also pregnant. I won't be able to help you."

"I'm calling to share the news, not to ask for help. You don't have to come here."

Despite the reactions I received from both moms, and Gautam's preoccupation with work, Bhavna and I were happy.

My friend, Crystal, advised me to be careful with Bhavna after the second baby's birth. "Make sure not to ignore her.

Sometimes the first child gets sad because she was the center of attention and suddenly mom focuses on the new baby."

I talked to Bhavna frequently. We were going to raise her brother or sister. "You'll have to help me with the baby."

During the second trimester, Sarojben, my mother-in-law and Ajay, Gautam's youngest brother visited.

When Gautam's parents came from India, they were in their late forties. His mother did not speak English. Dad was an attorney in India, which did not translate well in the American job market. To make ends meet, Gautam's mother worked in the kitchen of an Indian restaurant in downtown Berkeley. She loved cooking and won many prizes in competitions in India. She hoped to have an Indian restaurant of her own, one day.

Ajay, the youngest brother, was fifteen at the time. To help the family financially, he worked at the same restaurant as Mom. Making money at a young age, he lost interest in attending school. He also wanted to own a restaurant.

Since Gautam and I were the assumed financiers for the project, he insisted they open a restaurant near us. He grew up watching his parents lack the discipline needed to have a routine and orderly use of time and money. He believed Ajay and Mom needed guidance and supervision for the success of the project.

After going through the motions of exploring locations, availability of supplies, equipment and the potential for a busy customer flow, they decided to abandon the project. They returned to their lives. I got a feeling they did not want to leave the San Francisco Bay Area and move away from the rest of our family.

It was close to my due date. My mother-in-law called frequently to check if I was going to deliver on the due date which was the last week of May. During one such call, Gautam told her I was going to deliver any time. He said something that made her feel he needed her. She was with us shortly after the phone call.

A few days went by, but I was not getting contractions. Mom began to get impatient. She felt she was with us to help with Bhavna during the childbirth. Now she was wasting her vacation time.

She asked Gautam if the delivery could be induced so she could go back to work.

Gautam assured me it was not unusual to induce labor. It wouldn't affect the baby.

We were at the hospital, where a Burmese anesthesiologist, Thelma, our friend, was ready to administer the medication for inducing labor. She asked everyone, including Gautam, to leave the room. She turned to me with a stern face, asking why I had agreed to allow the inducement of labor.

"I don't know," I replied. "He said it was safe. My mother-in-law wants to go home."

Thelma was furious. "Just say no. Did you know your baby could go into distress?"

When she told me about the risks, I found the courage to refuse the process of inducing labor, even at the risk of upsetting my mother-in-law.

I told Sarojben, "Mom, you can go home if you have a problem at work."

She did not want to go back without finishing the job she was there for. I failed to understand why just the act of being home with Bhavna during the delivery was the only thing she cared about. But we spent a few more days together before the baby let me know it was time.

Early on Sunday, the seventh of June, I started having contractions.

Contrary to the large size of the Bronx hospital, the base

hospital was a small community with one doctor in each specialty. When I explained to my Ob/Gyn doctor about the trauma I felt during Bhavna's birth, he took tender care of me. He assured me the second experience of childbirth was going to be so easy it would make me forget the first one. I wasn't afraid.

After checking me, the doctor told us to go home and walk around the block a few times. Gautam and I walked around the neighborhood all day, resting periodically. Sometimes Bhavna joined us.

At the end of the day, we returned to the hospital. Bhavna stayed with my mother-in-law.

A beautiful boy was born a little after 11 pm.

We did not have a list of favorite names.

After one look at his gentle, calm eyes, we named him Shiv, which meant calm and stable in Gujarati. It was also the name of one of our widely worshiped Gods.

CHAPTER FORTY-FIVE

1987: PART 2

We came home with Shiv.

Bhavna couldn't wait to help me take care of her brother. During the day she made many trips to the bedroom to bring a fresh diaper and baby powder. I appreciated her help.

Gautam had one year left in his first tour of duty with the Air Force. He didn't want to sign up for a second tour and needed a place to relocate for a job or private practice. Often, he left home, to interview with hospitals in various locations or to check out potential places for private practice.

My mother-in-law, Saroj, cooked meals for us and tried to keep Bhavna busy. In a few days, my brother-in-law, Saurabh, called to invite Saroj to go to Reno with him and his wife, Asooya.

Saurabh made an offer Mom couldn't resist. She asked Gautam to book her a ticket to fly back to San Francisco.

Mom loved playing cards and going to the casinos. She and Dad drove to Reno frequently to play the slot machines. Dad didn't care to gamble so he dropped her off at the entrance. He checked into the hotel and spent time reading books in the room or a coffee shop. He was an avid reader, having no trouble finding things to read while she spent all of her time on the machines.

"I thought your boss was expecting you back at work," I told Mom.

"He won't know I'm not with you." Her eyes sparkled with a sense of cleverness.

I was afraid to be alone with both kids. Knowing Gautam would leave again, we tried to talk to her, but neither of us succeeded.

Before leaving, Sarojben suggested we sponsor her sister's son, Mahesh's wife Sadhna, to come to America. "If you need help, you can bring Sadhna from India. Maybe you can apply for a nanny-visa for her." Her suggestions wasn't the quick solution we needed. Just because we applied didn't mean it would happen right away.

I tried to organize my routines, but it did not work. Bhavna did not like taking naps. Shiv was a fussy baby and cried when I tried to feed him. I felt exhausted all the time. My postpartum depression added to the stress and anxiety.

Bhavna was bored. All the activities we did every day before Shiv was born had come to a halt. She felt lost and lonely.

One fine day she decided she needed to take matters into her own hands. At the time of the day we used to go to the park at the end of the street, she put on her shoes and left. When I looked for her in the house and didn't find her, I panicked. I looked in the backyard. Not there. I saw her walking on the street, halfway to the park.

I didn't know what to do. Should I leave Shiv and run after her? Should I take Shiv with me and then run after her? What if a car hits her while I'm trying to get Shiv? I was horrified. I left Shiv and brought her home.

Frustrated, angry, depressed and out of breath, I had only

one thought repeating in my brain. "Kill her. All your problems will go away. You can't take care of both. Shiv is too small. You'll have to kill her."

A small, rational part of my brain held me back. I called the crisis hotline on the base. "I want to kill my daughter. She is three years old and doesn't listen to me. I know it's wrong, but what else can I do?"

"Ma'am, calm down. You did the right thing. I'm glad you called us before you killed your daughter," the lady on the other end assured me. I felt better.

"Tell me who is in your family? Where is your husband? How old is your baby?" The kind lady asked me questions to learn what triggered my phone call.

At the end of a long conversation, she felt I'd recovered from the panic attack. She advised me that she would arrange for a teenage girl to come to our home every afternoon to play with Bhavna. The teenager would entertain and keep Bhavna busy while I rested.

The hotline advisor made me promise two things. One, to stay calm for the rest of the day, and two, to have the young girl come every day so I could rest. When she sensed I was calm, she had me promise one last thing before hanging up— to call them the minute I felt panic coming on.

Amy, the beautiful blonde teenager, became a regular at our home. She enjoyed Bhavna's energy and Bhavna loved having someone entertain her.

CHAPTER FORTY-SIX

1987: PART 3

The depression I felt after Shiv was born was similar to how I felt after Bhavna was born so I knew I had postpartum depression. The hormones had no sympathy for my situation and decided to stay longer which made me impatient and over reacting to every little thing. I needed to be upset at something for my feelings of doom. After eliminating the obvious ones, like my daughter and my husband, I decided to blame my hair. My hair was long and heavy and couldn't be easily controlled, making me feel as if dark clouds hung in front of me constantly.

After I came from India, I hadn't had the opportunity to learn about the finer things in life, especially about women's fashion and hairstyles.

One Saturday, while Gautam watched the kids, I went to the beauty shop.

"I want the hair in the front to go away from my face," I told the hairdresser.

"What do you mean?"

"All this hair that comes near my face makes me feel like they are dark clouds."

"You mean you want bangs?"

"Oh no," I said emphatically and with great fear. "Then, they'll never go away from my face."

"What do you want me to do?" the lady asked with exasperation.

"I've seen women with curly hair that never moves. Can you do that for me?"

"For a small curl, the hair has to be short."

"Oh." I thought about it for a few minutes and then asked, "Can you cut the front short and then curl it? That way, they won't fall on my face."

"Sure. Just to be clear, you want the rest of the hair to be left alone."

"Exactly." Finally she was getting it. "But, can you also cut the rest short?"

After two hours, I drove home with my tightly curled bangs. I entered the house and went straight to the bathroom to look at myself.

"Oh no." In shock, I decided to stay there forever. I had curly hair in the front that didn't move, as if it was stuck there. And the rest of the hair was the same. It looked weird and ugly. I never saw anyone looking like me before. What had I done?

My husband followed me to the bathroom. "Let me see."

"No, I look horrible. Why did I do this? It's all your fault. If you had helped me with our kids, I wouldn't be so depressed. Why did you let me go for this?" There was no stopping me from my hysterical raving.

"What did I do? Let me see. It can't be that bad."

"What do you know? It is horrible. I have to stay here until my hair grows back."

"Come on, you can't do that," he pleaded. "Our kids need you."

"Mommy, mommy, let me see," our daughter chirped.

After much crying, I opened the door.

She said innocently, "Hehe, you look funny, Mommy."

My husband knew better. After a few seconds of silence, with a straight face, he said, "You look great, different, but great."

"You're just saying that to appease me. You don't mean that."

"What did you tell her to do? Is this what you wanted?"

I burst into a new volley of tears. "I didn't know what I wanted or what to tell her."

"But she should understand. Let's go back to her. I'm going to tell her to fix this or I'm going to sue her."

"No, we can't do that. I'm embarrassed to even go out of the house. What if she is busy? Everyone there will see me."

After much arguing, we went to the beauty shop.

He thundered at the hairdresser. "What did you do to my wife's hair? You made her upset."

"Sir, calm down. This is what she wanted."

Puzzled, he looked at me and I nodded.

"Well, she didn't know. But you knew what it would look like." He kept going, but at a much lower intensity.

The hairdresser, a wise and kind lady, finally offered, "I can do another perm which can soften her tight curls so it looks better. Then we can wait for it to grow out."

He looked at me. Again, I nodded, gently but firmly.

After that I could look at myself in the mirror without crying.

CHAPTER FORTY-SEVEN
1987: PART 4

When Gautam returned from one of his interviews, I told him about my fear of harming Bhavna, and explained why we had a teenager in our home. He was sympathetic and concerned, but was also relieved I found a solution.

The incident made Gautam feel Bhavna was missing out on summer fun because of our circumstances. He wanted to do something nice for her and suggested we take her to Disneyland.

Shiv was barely two months old, which made me wonder if it was a good idea to take him into a crowded public place before his first immunization.

Gautam found a solution. "We can get him immunized before he is two months old. It's ok to do that."

"But why?" I argued. "We can go to Disneyland later. I am not in any condition to go there. Theme parks are tiring, even for a normal, healthy person. How will I manage with a newborn?"

"It will be fine. Bhavna needs this. Why don't you want your daughter to have fun? We can drive to San Francisco and pick up my parents. My mom can help you with Shiv."

Against my better instincts, we left for San Francisco.

I was hoping once we reached his parents' place, my mother-in-law would understand my hesitation and discomfort. She did not. She was ready to leave and hopped in the car before me. I was disappointed and felt neglected.

Disneyland in August was a hot place. Most of the time I sat in a shady area with Shiv while Gautam and Bhavna went on rides and had a great time. I was surprised how unafraid Bhavna was of the rides, even the ones scary to me.

We spent two full days in Disneyland, but the only two people who enjoyed it were Gautam and Bhavna. My in-laws didn't go on many rides and mostly hung around with me and Shiv. We took lots of pictures with Disney characters. When we were standing next to Winnie-The-Pooh, Shiv started crying. I loved Bhavna's spirit, she found joy everywhere.

That year we acquired our first computer. As the computer revolution picked up speed, the latest concept was the personal computer. Gautam's brother, Saurabh, who interned at IBM, helped Gautam purchase a computer for home use. Gautam spent much of his spare time learning to use it.

In December, my younger brother, Suresh, visited us from England. I enjoyed having long talks with him. We traveled back in time remembering how much fun we had growing up in India before he left for England. Gautam was perplexed at how much we giggled. I never saw Gautam relate to his brothers that way.

When I was busy with Shiv, Bhavna kept Suresh occupied.

The responsibility of sponsoring my brother and his family to come to America was always at the top of my mind. In anticipation of living in America for five years, Gautam and I applied for citizenship. Once the process was complete, we received an invitation to participate in the citizenship oath ceremony. The four of us traveled to Yakima, Washington to take the oath. We left early in the morning to make sure we had enough time to drive through the rain and snow.

My brother went with us and helped us with the kids while we went in for the oath ceremony. It was such an emotional experience. This one moment meant so many things to me, I felt overwhelmed. I would now be able to fulfill the responsibility of bringing my brother from India and make my parents happy. I had fallen in love with this country. I had a sense of gratitude for it. But I also felt I was betraying my beloved birth country. It was one of the most bittersweet moments of my life.

A few days later, we went to San Francisco with Suresh. My father-in-law was well-informed of the city's history because he loved to read. As a self-appointed tour guide, he took Suresh around. I stayed home with the children.

His dad struggled to find a job he'd be proud of. He worked as a caretaker for a quadriplegic male and in an airplane hanger, lying flat on scaffolding examining the ceiling of the hanger for hairline cracks. Later, between February and June 1982, he got a job as a caseworker at the Social Security Administration Office. He was proud of his new job and felt I brought him good luck as he got it after I married into their family.

They lived in an apartment in the less desirable part of Richmond, where the rent was affordable. Mom and Ajay, the youngest son, worked at an Indian restaurant while Saurabh, her middle son, attended Cal State Hayward.

On a recent job-seeking trip to San Francisco, Gautam stayed with his family. While there, his father's car was broken into and the radio was stolen. His dad laughed it off as a routine occurrence, but it bothered Gautam his parents and brothers had to live in such a risky neighborhood. He suggested they start looking for a home in a safe area.

Afraid they wouldn't have the money for the down payment, or even the monthly mortgage, they hesitated. But Gautam offered them funds from our savings for the down-payment, and also offered to pay half of the monthly mortgage. That's when they found a beautiful condo in Richmond near the Hilltop Mall. They were living there when we visited.

Gautam couldn't go sightseeing with his dad and Suresh, because we heard his cousin sister, Kamala's husband was seriously ill and was being airlifted from Visalia to Stanford Medical Center. He and his uncle drove to Stanford to be there for Kamala. I was glad being the only doctor in the family, he was there for them.

While Suresh and Dad toured the city, the children and I stayed with Saroj and Ajay. Saroj wanted to play cards, but the kids wouldn't leave us alone. I was not interested in cards. She insisted I give the kids a dose of Dimetapp to make them sleep so we could play. I didn't.

Upon returning from San Francisco, Suresh and I called our parents in India, a rare occurrence for our family because the three of us lived on three different continents. As usual, the conversation drifted towards the family dream of having us all in America. My parents also wanted me to arrange Suresh's marriage to an Indian girl so he'd leave the UK and move to the USA. There was no way they'd understand I didn't have the ability to accomplish it, and I didn't try to explain.

My brother shared with me, "They complain I don't visit them in India, and now you know why. These kinds of conversations discourage me. I feel uncomfortable. They don't understand me."

It was two days before Suresh was scheduled to fly out of Seattle when my first Indian friend, Hetal, called. I vented about the pressures I felt from my parents. "They want me to bring my older brother and his family here from India and now they want me to find a bride for Suresh. How am I going to do that? I don't know any Indian people."

"My uncle is looking for a match for his daughter," she said.

I told her Suresh didn't like the idea of arranged marriage and might get upset if I brought it up.

"We are not arranging. We are just suggesting. Let me find out from my uncle if he is interested. They know you, so I won't have to say much. You talk to your brother. You send your brother's picture and they'll send Dipa's picture. If they like what they see, we'll talk."

Suresh and Dipa looked at each other's pictures, talked on the phone, and my brother changed his flight from Seattle to Newark, New Jersey, instead of London. They were married within the year.

I was happy I fulfilled at least one of the two expectations of my parents.

CHAPTER FORTY-EIGHT
1988-PART 1

At home on the base, while giving Shiv a bath at the kitchen sink, I noticed a rash on his neck. I didn't think it was serious. I thought I'd have Gautam check it when he came home from work.

"Looks like eczema. He has dry skin. Put some Vaseline on it."

I followed his instructions but the rash did not go away. Worried, I took him to the pediatrician and got the same response as my husband's. He recommended using 1% hydrocortisone cream until the rash cleared up. He assured me infantile eczema was common and usually cleared up within six months.

As days went by, I noticed more rashes on Shiv's body. He also started scratching the rash with his tiny little hands. He became more irritable and uneasy.

"What's wrong with him?" I'd ask Gautam.

"Nothing is wrong with him. He has dry skin and eczema. Keep his skin hydrated. Don't worry."

Shiv started waking up at night, crying and scratching. To prevent him from hurting himself, I began sleeping with him.

The moment I felt him fidgeting, I'd rub sensitive areas of skin to soothe him back to sleep.

I asked my mother about Indian remedies. She suggested I boil *neem leaves* in oil and use the oil on his skin. I didn't know where to get neem leaves. We tried keeping his hands in cotton mittens to prevent him from scratching. He did not like that at all and screamed until we took them off. I put them on after he fell asleep to keep him from scratching during the night.

Itching, scratching, putting more hydrocortisone and Vaseline on his rashes became a part of our lives.

Six months passed and nothing changed. The pediatrician said sometimes infantile eczema lasted longer. We should wait another six months before testing him for other causes. We managed.

The base was close to Canada. Gautam wanted to take advantage of the proximity to the Rockies before we left the base for good.

His parents loved to travel so Gautam invited them to join us on a trip to see the glaciers in Banff National Park and the Canadian Rockies. Gautam planned the itinerary and his parents and his brother, Saurabh, and his wife, Asooya, joined us.

We enjoyed the trip. I loved walking on the glaciers. I felt like I was experiencing the universe, something bigger than me. Bhavna had the best time. She had so much curiosity and courage. She wasn't afraid of walking on the slippery glaciers. She was full of questions and tried to engage Uncle Saurabh, but that didn't work. He was busy with Asooya.

Gautam requested his parents to watch Bhavna and Shiv while he and I took a rafting trip. I was afraid of water but Gautam assured me the tour company would provide us with the proper gear to keep us from drowning. The raft bumping over the rough waters was quite scary, but I managed by screaming at every turn.

Gautam's term of service was ending on July 18th. We had to move out, clean the house, get it inspected after required corrections, and turn it over. Fortunately, the movers came and packed everything. The boxes and furniture would stay in storage until we needed them.

"Can I throw away the medical journals and magazines? They are old. We brought them here from New York because you wanted to read them and tear out your favorite articles for your collection, but you didn't even touch them in three years."

"No. I'm going to do that. I want to keep those magazines. What is your problem?"

"I don't have a problem. It's just you never looked at them. Besides, doesn't medical science keep evolving? The information may be obsolete now."

We took boxes of magazines- *Archives of General Surgery, Journal of American Medical Association, American Journal of Surgery*, and more.

Bhavna loved drawing with crayons on the walls. I tried to stop her, but her dad thought I was stunting her creativity. When the base officers came to inspect the house, they suggested we remove the crayon marks from the walls. I avoided looking at Gautam. He told the inspectors he tried many ways to remove them but nothing had worked. They suggested he try harder. They'd return.

On July 18th, Bhavna, Shiv and I stayed at the base hotel, while Gautam worked late into the night, removing the crayon stains.

The next day, while waiting for him to finish the final paperwork, Shiv's body temperature rose to 103 degrees. I rushed him to the emergency room. The doctor filled up the sink with cold water and put Shiv in it. He was cranky from the discomfort of the fever and started bawling. With his arms stretched towards me, he tried to get out. I stood back with Bhavna, ready to cry.

Once the fever came down, they took him out of the freezing sink water and handed him to me. I quickly dried him and put his clothes back on him. After giving us instructions, they let us go home.

At home, I gave him baby Tylenol. The fever kept getting lower. I had to repeat that a few times before the fever stopped completely. We never understood what caused the sudden fever, but I was thankful he was better.

CHAPTER FORTY-NINE
SAN FRANCISCO, CA 1988: PART 2

On July 19th, we filled Gautam's car, the Accord, with personal items we kept with us - our clothing, Shiv's high chair, stroller, and toys, along with Bhavna's books and toys. I drove the Nissan, with Shiv in the infant car seat and Bhavna next to him to keep him entertained. Spokane to San Francisco was going to be a long drive.

We stayed at a hotel one night and reached Gautam's parents' condo by the evening of the following day.

Before going to work, my mother-in-law, Saroj, had prepared dinner. Dad, Babubhai, was home to receive us. His cheerful demeanor was welcoming. Despite our protest, Saroj and Babubhai moved into the second, smaller bedroom so the four of us would be comfortable in the master bedroom.

The very next day, Gautam went for an interview he scheduled with Kaiser Hospital in Richmond. Someone from the hospital informed him they needed a surgeon urgently, when he called. However, upon reaching there, someone from the hospital told him they had no need for a general surgeon. He returned home, disappointed.

In the following few days, he experienced more rejections.

His interactions at the places he visited gave him the impression he was being discriminated against due to his ethnicity.

I wanted my children to be around extended family so I continued to insist he join a group of surgeons or a hospital to work for.

On the other hand, Gautam believed he had made enough attempts to find employment, despite his strong aversion to working for someone. He was getting impatient and believed it was time for him to find a place to practice.

About the time he felt frustrated and hopeless, his cousin Kamala called from Visalia. Her husband, who practiced Radiology in Visalia, passed away six months earlier when we were visiting with my brother. She was looking for a doctor to continue evaluating worker's compensation patients for disability. She suggested while helping her, he'd get a chance to explore Visalia as a permanent location to practice. Gautam went there to check it out.

Once in Visalia, he visited Kaweah Delta Hospital to discuss the potential of starting a surgery practice. The staff in the administration office wanted to know if a group in Visalia was recruiting him. When he said, "No," they refused to give him the application for hospital privileges.

Kamala suggested he visit Visalia Community Hospital, where he met Dr. Jagatik. Due to a shortage of surgeons, it was common for primary care physicians and even pathologists to perform minor surgical procedures. Dr. Jagatik, a pathologist, was one such doctor. Wanting to retire, he offered to rent his office space to Gautam for $6000 per month and expected Gautam would purchase his practice. We did not have the money to accept his offer.

Kamala told him to visit Springfield and meet with one of her husband's friends, Prakash Patel. Dr. Patel, an anesthesiologist, forwarded him to Dr. Pindhara, an Internist. That evening, Gautam went to see him at his home.

Dr. Pindhara encouraged him to start his surgical practice in Springfield. He informed Gautam about the status of surgery services. There was an older surgeon, Dr. Esteban, who'd been in Springfield since before Dr. Pindhara arrived. According to Dr. Pindhara, this surgeon had a combative attitude, making it difficult for the primary care doctors to refer patients to him. There was another surgeon, Dr. Jean, who was good, but very busy. Dr. Pindhara believed one more surgeon was necessary and would be good for the community.

That evening, an Indian pharmacist was hosting a birthday party for his son. All the Indian community would be there. Gautam was invited to the party to meet everyone.

Gautam received positive feedback at the party. He felt encouraged to settle down in Springfield. He felt he had found a mentor and a guide in Dr. Pindhara.

After one more visit to Springfield, Gautam came back to us with the keys to an office and a house.

CHAPTER FIFTY

SPRINGFIELD, CA 1988: PART 3

I wasn't sure what to feel. Should I be happy he found a place to practice? Or, should I be upset we'd be far from family? My deep sense of insecurity about money made me concerned we did not have money to start the practice. My anger for him awakened as I was reminded of the fact he had used up our savings to help purchase the condo his parents lived in.

"How will we start a business? We have no money." I verbalized my concerns as we sat around the dining table at his parents' condo. "We won't be able to hire anyone."

"Mom, it would be nice if you came to help, in the beginning," Gautam requested Saroj.

She took no time to respond. "I have a job. I can't." Looking at me, she added, "You are educated, you can help him."

"But, what about the kids? I don't know anyone in Springfield. How will I find a babysitter? Settling down in a new place takes time. How will I do both? Set up home and business?"

Reluctantly, his mom offered. "I can come to Springfield to help you with the home and children until your practice is settled."

Surprised, Gautam wanted to make sure she understood medical business was not like other businesses, where you get paid at the time of providing service or even before doing so. "Once I start, it will be a few months before the insurance companies will pay for what I have done for the patients. So, you'd have to stay longer than a month."

Always a card player, she thought about her options, and made a proposition. "How about I come for six months? Would that be enough? And then, you can give me money to start my restaurant."

"Sure, not a problem." Gautam looked relieved. He looked towards me and asked, "Would that work for you?"

"As long as my young kids are taken care of I am fine."

Unknown what the future had in stock for us, we drove out to Springfield.

I was surprised at Gautam's quick decision and a little disappointed as well. I didn't have a chance to visit Springfield before he decided. Springfield seemed too far from his family.

I felt sick we'd have to make a deal so the family's first two grandchildren would be taken care of, especially when the condo we were sitting in was purchased without any promises to us in return.

We left for Springfield after that. The Air Force delivered the belongings to our rental home and we opened for business on August 8, 1988.

CHAPTER FIFTY-ONE

1988: PART 4

The rental house in Springfield was similar to the house we'd lived in on the base. It had three bedrooms, one big living room, and a good-sized kitchen with a nook for a dining table.

The next day, we went to see the office Gautam rented for practice at 560 W. Putnam Avenue, Suite 9. It was in a small single-story L-shaped office complex near the hospital. It had four small exam rooms, a small front office, one bathroom in the hallway, and a reasonably large office with an attached bathroom for the staff. The waiting area had room for eight chairs.

Before leaving for the office, we looked at the *Choghadiya* to determine the auspicious time to enter and do the opening. It is one of the simplest ways to find out the auspicious time in a particular day. As per Vedic Astrology, the time is calculated in *Ghadi* which are each 24 minutes. So, *Chaughadiya* is of approximately 96 minutes duration.

At the appropriate time, we put a small heap of rice on the counter of one exam room. On it, we set a brass container half-filled with water. On top of the brass vessel, we placed a coconut, a symbol of good luck and prosperity. In front of the heap of rice, we placed a plate with *kumkum* flowers and *divo*, a small silver container with a cotton wick dipped in ghee. We had Bhavna light the *divo* because a young unmarried girl is believed to bring good luck to her parents' family. We sang a short *shloka* for Lord Ganesha, the remover of obstacles. Now we were ready to start.

Cousin Kamala sold us waiting room chairs, an IBM Selectric typewriter, and one flat bright orange exam table. After her husband died suddenly she moved to the Bay Area with her boys.

Gautam prepared a proposal to apply for a bank loan. First, we applied at a local community bank that was started in Springfield. They rejected our application because we did not have a history of running a successful business and assets for collateral. We weren't discouraged. We went to a branch of a national bank. Although not as blunt and dismissive as the local bank, the manager at this bank also rejected our application. He explained he didn't have the authority to approve a loan for the amount of money we needed.

Delivered by the Air Force, the house was littered with boxes. Saroj was watching the kids during the day and was getting impatient because of the unavailability of certain household items. Shiv, barely a year old, was showing signs of stress from being in a new place and not being with me all day. He cried a lot.

We went to a local branch of another national bank chain. The manager had a kind face. The gentle demeanor about him made us feel comfortable being there. He looked over the proposal.

"Your needs are beyond my authority. I'm sorry."

Gautam responded, "You are the third person to say this. We have no history and no assets. If I don't get a chance how am I going to establish and prove myself? The Air Force didn't pay much."

"You were in the Air Force? So was I. I am a Vietnam vet."

"I didn't owe the US Government anything and didn't need to join. But, I left the Air Force because I wasn't able to do the number of cases I preferred and the slow pace of life frustrated me. "If someone would help me get started, I'm here to establish my surgery practice."

"Well, I am sure you'll do well. But the amount you are requesting is beyond my level of authority."

The manager sensed our frustration. "Here's what I can do for you," he said, smiling. "I can't approve your request for a loan but I have the power to offer you a line of credit for $15,000. As a fellow Air Force veteran, I'm willing to do that if you think you can make it work."

Although afraid and embarrassed to look ignorant, we asked him to explain what a line of credit meant. When he finished explaining, we were thrilled.

Excited, Gautam clarified, "So, if we don't use the money we don't have to pay interest? This is even better than a loan."

In the next few days, we purchased minimal surgical instruments, two more exam tables, a peg-board accounting system that Kamalaben suggested, a box of patient charts, and a box of Form 1500 to be used for billing insurance after Gautam started seeing patients. Later, Kamalaben taught me how to use the pegboard system for keeping track of daily income.

Gautam was obviously more familiar with the business of medicine. He mentioned things like billing codes, insurance contracts, Medicare and Medicaid, co-pays and co-insurances, referrals, and the assignment of benefits. I understood none of these and soon realized he didn't either. He just knew the jargon.

I made phone calls to places that might have answers. "Hello, I'm calling from Dr. Pandit's office. What is a contract? And, can we have one?" I asked the Blue Cross lady who answered the phone.

"Are you in a practice?"

"Not yet."

"Does the doctor have a California license? Is he enrolled in Medicare?"

Aha, we need a California license. "Gautam, do you have a license to practice in California?"

"Of course."

In the application forms for contracts, there was a "yes or no" box asking if we had a business license. I called the insurance company. "Why are there two boxes for the same thing? I already wrote the California License number in one box."

"Yes, but you need a business license."

"Isn't it the same? License is for permission to practice. We have that."

"You don't get it. Call the city hall."

"What is a city hall?"

"Look in the phone book and find the number for the city hall. You'll see. Call them."

Gradually, by asking dumb questions and making many mistakes, we were contracted with Blue Cross, Blue Shield, and enrolled in Medicare and Medicaid.

At home, though, things were not going so well. Mom seemed sad and upset all the time. Four-year-old Bhavna told me, "Mommy, Ba-mummy (that's what she called her) was crying today."

"Mom, are you ok?"

"I was talking to a Gujarati lady today. She said you could hire a babysitter to stay with the children for $500 per month."

"We don't have $500 to spare."

"Also, the lady was saying you should host a dinner for the Indian doctors, otherwise they will not send patients to Gautam."

The unpacking was not finished. I was working five days a week to help Gautam get started. There was not enough money to sustain ourselves. And now I had to host a dinner. My naïve mind did not understand why being a good surgeon was not enough.

Nevertheless, we made good progress in a month.

Gautam's dad came to visit one weekend. We noticed Mom was packed. There was no indication or conversation she was planning to leave with Dad until then, which surprised and scared me.

"Mom, you are leaving?"

Always a woman of few words, she gave a short answer. "Yes."

"What about the restaurant you want to open?" Gautam asked her, almost teasing her.

"I'll be back for that."

I was upset. My dad always used to tell me I felt things very strongly and needed to learn not to react so intensely.

"What will I do with the kids? Who'll watch them?"

She was ready with an answer, "Call that lady. Or sponsor my sister's son's family to come from India. He can work in your office and his wife can work as a housekeeper. They have two boys. They can go to school with your children."

The nephew and his wife did not speak English. Mom expected us to pay salaries to him and his wife and have them stay with us, help them with their kids, and even pay for their four tickets to come from India.

Gautam thought that was a great idea. "See, my mom has found a solution for us. Should we start the paperwork?"

I was flabbergasted by the outrageousness of the idea. Immigration sponsorship takes time, so we'd still have to hire a babysitter. While I needed help with my two children, he was considering having an eight-person household. No one saw the absurdity of the proposition, and the havoc it would wreak on our family, and for me personally. I refused to go down this potentially treacherous path. Time will tell whether I made the right decision.

ACKNOWLEDGMENTS

I am grateful to my parents. It is true everything we try to do or are able to do, and the opportunities available to us, depend on where we are born. So, yes, I am thankful to my parents, Navnit and Yashoda. They didn't have much but whatever they had they gave, most of all their values of dreaming big and working hard for their dreams, of not hurting others intentionally, and of good education. My father's vision and forward-thinking nature, desire to make a better life for himself and his family, and my mother's "can do" attitude were exemplary. Thank you, Mom and Dad.

I thank my writing group I found by accident. And what a wonderful accident it was. Shirley Hickman, Marilyn Meredith, Brent Gill, Dr. Rao, Jann McGuire, and Debbie Ecobiza, all accepted me with open arms and thus began my journey of learning to write. They made me realize there was a story I should tell and encouraged me along the way.

I am grateful for the timely editing help I received from Joan Raymond, a published author, a coach, and an editor for holding my hand through the process of getting the books to you.

I thank the very creative designer of my book cover, Kalakaar Rekha Ratnam. I loved what she came up with.

I thank my beta readers, Mickie Manning, Barbara Swartzel, Charlene Thomas, Jean Vafeadas, Suzie DeBar, and… who took time to make my book better.

And lastly, to my readers, I thank you for reading my book. Because of your support, I will continue to write the stories of my life.

ABOUT THE AUTHOR

Ela Pandya was born in India and moved to America when her parents arranged her marriage to an Indian doctor doing surgery residency in New York City. Highly educated, she was restless to make a career in her new country. She faced challenges in her life due to cultural expectations of her own family and her husband's cultural expectations due to gender stereotypes, as a general surgeon's wife and has made a good life for herself.

She has lived in California for thirty-four years, raised two kids to be decent human beings, and pursued her passion for gender equality.

eBook readers, please click on the image above to go to my website. Print books users: https://elapandya.com

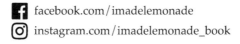

facebook.com/imadelemonade
instagram.com/imadelemonade_book

ALSO BY ELA PANDYA

Made in the USA
Monee, IL
14 November 2023

46472896R10146